MathFlare

Name: ___________________________

Class: ___________

Teacher: ___________________________

Introduction

As parents and educators, we recognize the pivotal role mathematics plays in shaping a child's academic journey and future success. Yet, the path to mathematical proficiency can often seem daunting, fraught with challenges and complexities. That's where the transformative power of MathFlare Workbooks shine through, illuminating the way forward with clarity, precision, and purpose.

Introducing MathFlare Workbooks – a beacon of guidance, a testament to excellence, and a catalyst for achievement. Crafted with meticulous care and expertise, MathFlare Workbooks stand as paragons of educational excellence, designed to nurture young minds, ignite a passion for learning, and develop a deep-rooted understanding of mathematical concepts.

Picture this: your child eagerly delves into the pages of Mathflare Workbook, greeted by a step-by-step guide illuminated with vivid examples that demystify complex mathematical concepts. With each turn of the page, they embark on a journey of discovery, encountering thoughtfully curated practice questions that reinforce learning and hone problem-solving skills. And when they unveil the answers to those very questions, a sense of accomplishment blossoms within them – a tangible reward for their hard work and dedication.

But MathFlare Workbooks are more than just tools for learning; they are pathways to comprehension, fostering a deep-seated understanding of mathematical concepts through a sequential, logical flow. From fundamental principles to advanced problem-solving strategies, every chapter builds upon the last, ensuring a robust foundation upon which future knowledge can be constructed.

As parents, we yearn for nothing more than to see our children thrive, to witness the spark of inspiration ignited within them as they conquer academic challenges with confidence and poise. MathFlare Workbooks serve as partners in this noble endeavor, offering not just practice questions, but the keys to unlocking a world of opportunity.

And for teachers, MathFlare Workbooks stand as invaluable allies in the quest to cultivate mathematical proficiency in the classroom. With answers readily available, instructors can focus on guiding and nurturing their students, confident in the knowledge that MathFlare Workbooks provide a solid framework upon which to build.

In the pages of MathFlare Workbooks, we find not just the promise of academic excellence, but the seeds of a brighter tomorrow. So let us embrace the power of mathematics, let us champion the journey of learning, and let us pave the way for a generation of young minds poised to shape the world. With MathFlare Workbooks as our guide, the possibilities are infinite, and the future, bright.

Table of Contents

MathFlare
MATH WORKBOOK
Grade 2
Addition Subtraction
Multiplication
Place Value and Expanded Notations
Geometry
Step by Step Guide and Essential Practice with Answers
MathFlare Publishing

MathFlare
MATH WORKBOOK
Grade 2-3
Addition Subtraction
Multiplication and Division
Place Value and Expanded Notations
Geometry
Step by Step Guide and Essential Practice with Answers
MathFlare Publishing

MathFlare
MATH WORKBOOK
Grade 3
Multiplication and Division
Decimals
Place Value and Expanded Notations
Fractions and Geometry
Step by Step Guide and Essential Practice with Answers
MathFlare Publishing

MathFlare
MATH WORKBOOK
Grade 1
Counting and Numbers
Addition and Subtraction
Place Value and Expanded Notations
Understanding Time
Step by Step Guide and Essential Practice with Answers
MathFlare Publishing

MathFlare
MATH WORKBOOK
Grade 1-2
Counting and Numbers
Addition and Subtraction
Place Value and Expanded Notations
Understanding Time
Step by Step Guide and Essential Practice with Answers
MathFlare Publishing

MathFlare
MATH WORKBOOK
Grade 3-4
Addition Subtraction
Multiplication Division
Place Value and Expanded Notations
Fractions and Geometry
Step by Step Guide and Essential Practice with Answers
MathFlare Publishing

MathFlare
MATH WORKBOOK
Grade 4
Addition Subtraction
Multiplication Division
Place Value and Expanded Notations
Fractions and Geometry
Step by Step Guide and Essential Practice with Answers
MathFlare Publishing

MathFlare
MATH WORKBOOK
Grade 4-5
Multiplication Division
Place Value and Expanded Notations
Fractions and Geometry
Unit Conversion
Step by Step Guide and Essential Practice with Answers
MathFlare Publishing

MathFlare
MATH WORKBOOK
Grade 5
Step by Step Guide and Essential Practice with Answers
Multiplication Division
Place Value and Expanded Notations
Fractions and Geometry
Unit Conversion
MathFlare Publishing

MathFlare
MATH WORKBOOK
Grade 5-6
Step by Step Guide and Essential Practice with Answers
Multiplication Division
Place Value and Expanded Notations
Fractions and Geometry
Units and Statistics
MathFlare Publishing

MathFlare
MATH WORKBOOK
Grade 6
Step by Step Guide and Essential Practice with Answers
Integers and Statistics
Arithmetic and Pre-Algebra
Fractions and Geometry
Ratio and Percentage
MathFlare Publishing

MathFlare
MATH WORKBOOK
Grade 6-7
Step by Step Guide and Essential Practice with Answers
Arithmetic and Pre-Algebra
Ratio, Percent Proportion
Geometry
Statistics
MathFlare Publishing

MathFlare
MATH WORKBOOK
Grade 7
Step by Step Guide and Essential Practice with Answers
Pre-Algebra
Ratio, Percent Proportion
Geometry
Statistics
MathFlare Publishing

MathFlare
MATH WORKBOOK
Grade 7-8
Step by Step Guide and Essential Practice with Answers
Pre-Algebra
Ratio, Percent Proportion
Geometry and Cartesian Plane
Statistics
MathFlare Publishing

MathFlare
MATH WORKBOOK
Grade 8-9
Step by Step Guide and Essential Practice with Answers
Pre-Algebra
Ratio, Proportion and Percentage
Linear Equations
Geometry and Cartesian Plane
MathFlare Publishing

MathFlare
MATH WORKBOOK
Grade 8
Step by Step Guide and Essential Practice with Answers
Pre-Algebra
Percentage
Linear Equations
Geometry
MathFlare Publishing

Place Value and Rounding Numbers

Place value tells us the value of a digit in a number based on where it's placed.

Imagine we have the number 87,647.528. It has 6 digits.

Now, each digit holds a special place. Let's break down the number 87,647.528:

- The digit 8 is in the ten thousands place. Its value is 8×10000=80000.

- The digit 7 is in the thousands place. Its value is 7×1000=7000.

- The digit 6 is in the hundreds place. Its value is 6×100=600.

- The digit 4 is in the tens place. Its value is 4×10=40.

- The digit 7 is in the ones place. Its value is 7×1=7.

- The digit 5 is in the tenths place. Its value is $5 \times \frac{1}{10} = 0.5$.

- The digit 2 is in the hundredths place. Its value is $2 \times \frac{1}{100} = 0.02$.

- The digit 8 is in the thousandths place. Its value is $8 \times \frac{1}{1000} = 0.008$.

When we add these values together, we find the value of the entire number:

$$80000 + 7000 + 600 + 40 + 7 + 0.5 + 0.02 + 0.008 = 87,647.528$$

Let's solve some problems:

Place value of the underlined digit:

$$3{,}7\underline{9}7.455 = \underline{\quad 7 \text{ hundreds} \quad}$$

Expanded notations:

37,311.07	30,000 + 7,000 + 300 + 10 + 1 + 0.07
2,514.153	2 thousands + 5 hundreds + 1 ten + 4 ones + 1 tenth + 5 hundredths + 3 thousandths
67,039.04	6 ten thousands + 7 thousands + 3 tens + 9 ones + 4 hundredths

Rounding Numbers

Rounding numbers is the process of approximating a numerical value to a certain degree of accuracy by replacing it with a simpler or more convenient value. Rounding is commonly used to simplify calculations and express numbers in a more manageable form.

Steps to Rounding Numbers:

1. **Identify the digit to be rounded:** Determine the digit to which the number will be rounded.

2. **Look at the next digit:** Examine the digit immediately to the right of the one being rounded.

3. **Decide whether to round up or down:** If the next digit is 5 or greater, round the digit up. If it is less than 5, round the digit down.

4. **Adjust the number:** Change the digit being rounded and replace all digits to the right with zeros if necessary.

Properties of Rounding Numbers:

1. **Accuracy:** Rounding reduces the precision of a number but maintains its approximate value.

2. **Simplicity:** Rounding simplifies calculations by using fewer digits.

3. **Ease of Use:** Rounding makes numbers easier to work with, especially in mental arithmetic and estimation.

Methods of Rounding Numbers:

1. **Round to Nearest Integer:** Round to the nearest whole number.

    I.   Round Up (Ceiling): Always round up to the nearest integer.
    II. Round Down (Floor): Always round down to the nearest integer.

2. **Round to Nearest Tenth:** Round to the nearest tenth (one decimal place).

3. **Round to Nearest Hundredth:** Round to the nearest hundredth (two decimal places).

4. **Round to Nearest Thousandth:** Round to the nearest thousandth (three decimal places).

5. **Round to Specific Decimal Places:** Round to a specified number of decimal places as needed.

Let's round the number **438,576.214** to various degrees of accuracy:

Rounding Level	Rounded Number	Difference from Original
Nearest Whole Number	438,576	0
Nearest Ten	438,580	+4
Nearest Hundred	438,600	+24
Nearest Thousand	439,000	+424
Nearest Ten Thousand	440,000	+3,424
Nearest Hundred Thousand	400,000	−38,576
Nearest Million	0.4386×10^6	−438,576.214

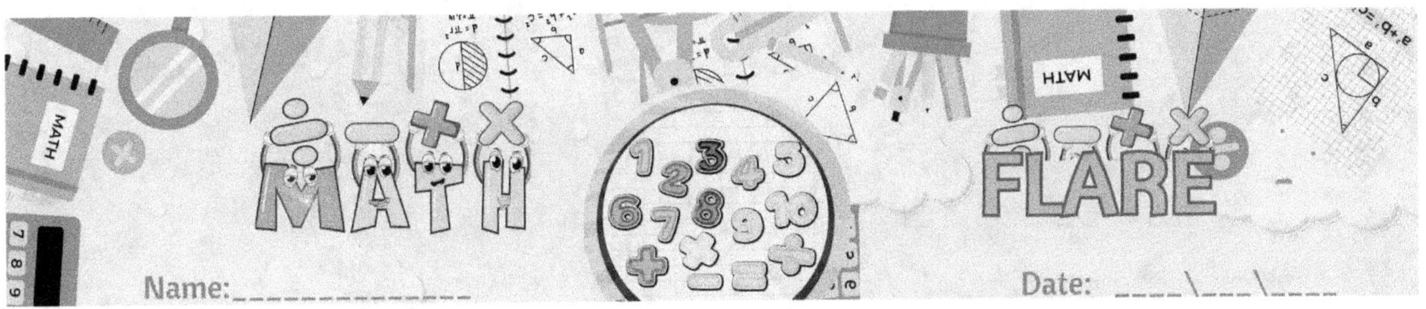

Place Value

Determine the place value of the underlined digit.

1. 426,902.54 = _______________________________

2. 626,622.83 = _______________________________

3. 566,482.34 = _______________________________

4. 799,482.73 = _______________________________

5. 622,254.96 = _______________________________

6. 304,654.85 = _______________________________

7. 520,451.72 = _______________________________

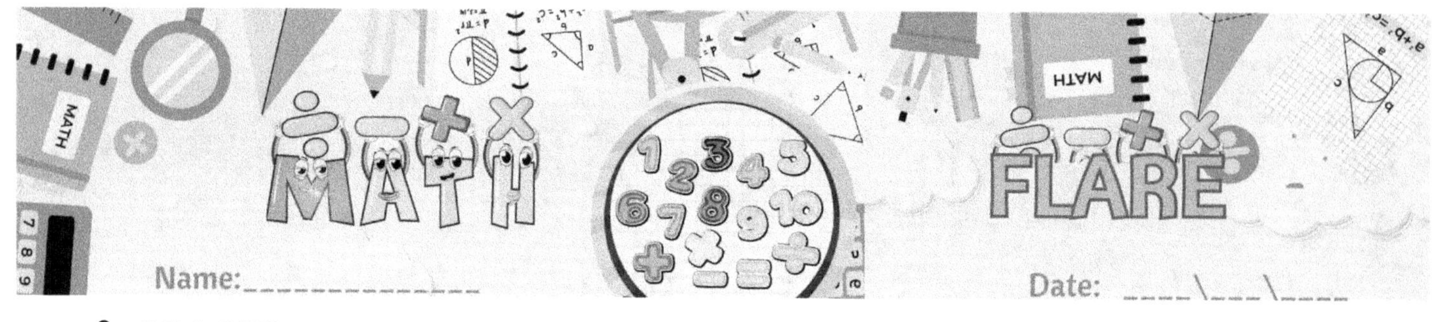

8. 936,07<u>7</u> = _______________________________

9. 197,<u>0</u>12.13 = _______________________________

10. 499,<u>5</u>20.63 = _______________________________

11. 121,86<u>1</u>.83 = _______________________________

12. 114,<u>0</u>00.39 = _______________________________

13. 958,5<u>0</u>5.5 = _______________________________

14. <u>7</u>48,874.75 = _______________________________

15. 478,60<u>6</u>.49 = _______________________________

16. 819,2_73.35 = ______________________________

17. 2_16,224 = ______________________________

18. _460,991.69 = ______________________________

19. 547,56_0.51 = ______________________________

20. 455,033._94 = ______________________________

21. 322,1_05.42 = ______________________________

22. 874,470._19 = ______________________________

23. 706,5_85.65 = ______________________________

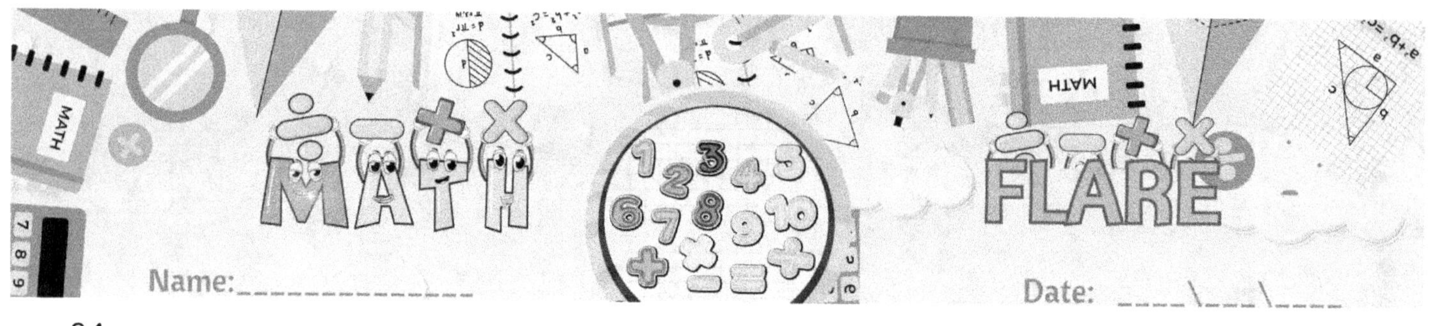

24. 127,472.34 = _______________________________

25. 540,538.95 = _______________________________

26. 975,774.14 = _______________________________

27. 832,868.74 = _______________________________

28. 894,616.04 = _______________________________

29. 918,373.24 = _______________________________

30. 814,758.65 = _______________________________

31. 745,247.19 = _______________________________

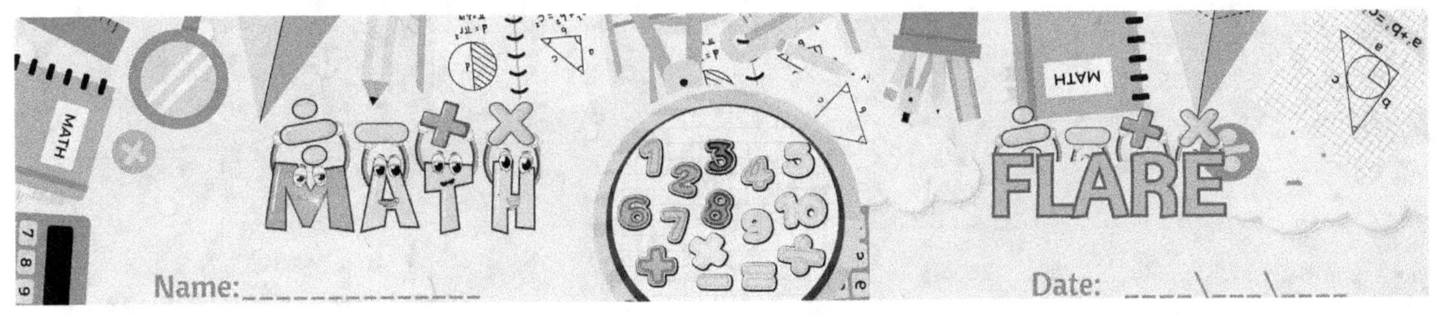

32. 438,854.6<u>4</u> = _______________________________________

33. 331,<u>0</u>57.22 = _______________________________________

34. 519,02<u>4</u>.87 = _______________________________________

35. 467,970.<u>4</u> = _______________________________________

36. 40<u>3</u>,038.42 = _______________________________________

37. 267,<u>8</u>80.41 = _______________________________________

38. 352,<u>3</u>11.71 = _______________________________________

39. 843,804.<u>6</u>2 = _______________________________________

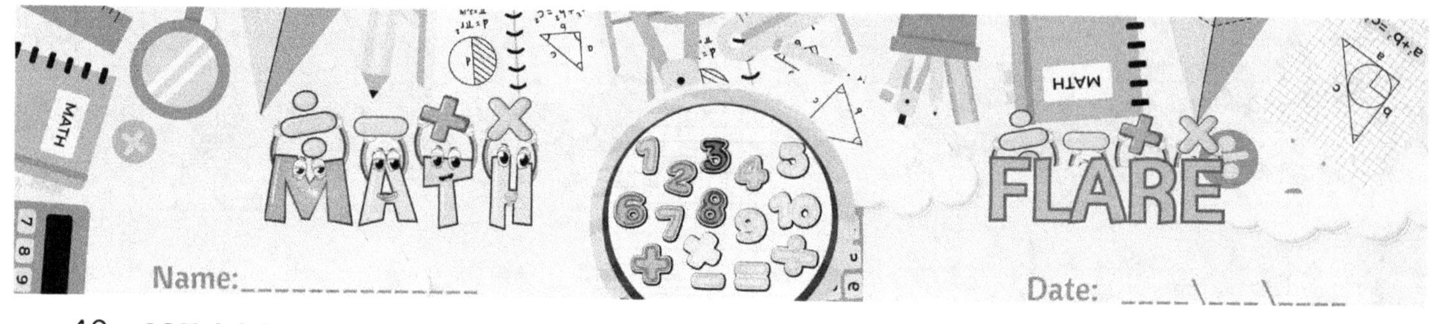

40. 697,829.<u>4</u>4 = _______________________________________

41. 852,6<u>0</u>7.43 = _______________________________________

42. 902,1<u>7</u>0.43 = _______________________________________

43. 263,082.1<u>3</u> = _______________________________________

44. 3<u>4</u>8,738.04 = _______________________________________

45. 2<u>9</u>9,026.1 = _______________________________________

46. 744,2<u>1</u>9.39 = _______________________________________

47. 699,101.<u>6</u>2 = _______________________________________

Place Value: Expanded Notation

Provide the expanded notation for each value.

48. _________________________ 5 thousands + 2 hundreds + 7 tens + 9 tenths + 7 hundredths

49. _________________________ 2 thousands + 5 hundreds + 1 ten + 2 ones + 7 tenths + 3 hundredths

50. _________________________ 1 thousand + 9 hundreds + 6 tens + 3 ones + 4 tenths + 4 hundredths

51. _________________________ 1 thousand + 8 tens + 6 ones + 6 tenths + 2 hundredths

52. _________________________ 8 thousands + 4 hundreds + 1 ten + 2 tenths + 5 hundredths

53. _________________________ 5 thousands + 6 hundreds + 2 tens + 1 one + 8 tenths

54. _________________________ 7 thousands + 1 hundred + 5 ones + 6 tenths + 3 hundredths

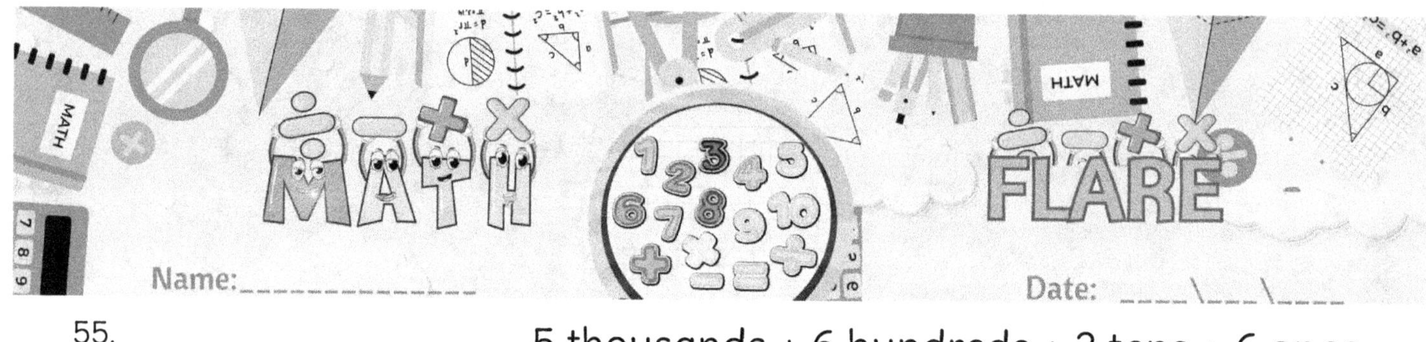

Name:_______________________   Date: ____________

55. _________________________ 5 thousands + 6 hundreds + 2 tens + 6 ones + 2 tenths + 4 hundredths

56. _________________________ 3 thousands + 6 hundreds + 9 tens + 7 ones + 9 tenths + 9 hundredths

57. _________________________ 3 thousands + 2 hundreds + 6 ones + 2 tenths + 9 hundredths

58. _________________________ 9 thousands + 6 hundreds + 5 tens + 9 ones + 3 tenths

59. _________________________ 3 thousands + 2 hundreds + 1 ten + 8 ones + 4 tenths + 3 hundredths

60. _________________________ 3 thousands + 3 tens + 6 tenths + 2 hundredths

61. _________________________ 1 thousand + 5 hundreds + 3 tens + 3 ones + 1 tenth

62. _________________________ 3 thousands + 4 hundreds + 5 tens + 1 one + 5 tenths + 7 hundredths

63. __________________ 2 thousands + 5 hundreds + 6 ones + 5 tenths + 6 hundredths

64. __________________ 4 thousands + 4 hundreds + 9 tens + 5 tenths + 2 hundredths

65. __________________ 4 thousands + 6 hundreds + 5 tens + 3 ones + 6 tenths + 6 hundredths

66. __________________ 6 thousands + 9 hundreds + 2 tens + 5 ones + 6 tenths + 6 hundredths

67. __________________ 9 thousands + 2 hundreds + 2 tens + 5 ones + 3 tenths + 1 hundredth

68. __________________ 8 thousands + 7 hundreds + 5 ones + 4 tenths + 3 hundredths

69. __________________ 4 thousands + 1 hundred + 9 tens + 8 ones + 5 tenths + 4 hundredths

70. __________________ 6 thousands + 2 hundreds + 3 tens + 6 ones + 7 tenths + 8 hundredths

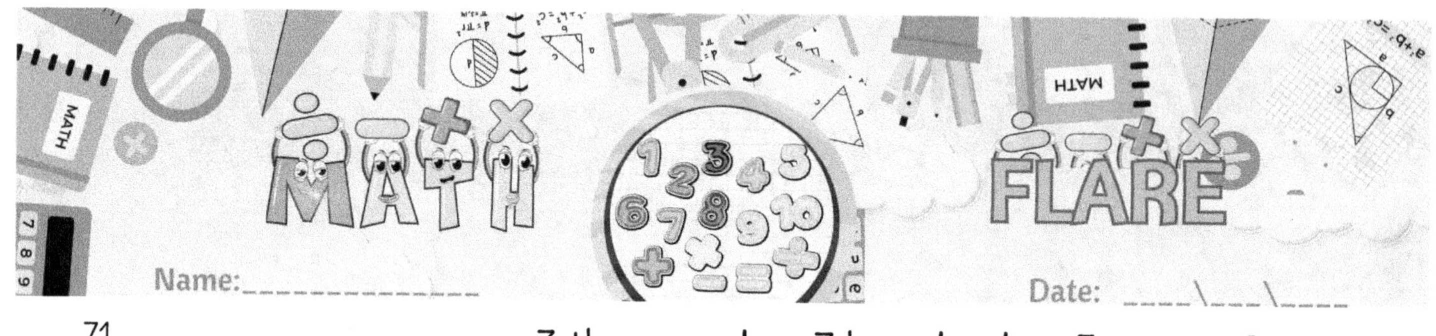

71. _______________________ 3 thousands + 7 hundreds + 5 tens + 6 ones + 4 tenths + 5 hundredths

72. _______________________ 5 thousands + 3 hundreds + 5 tens + 4 ones + 5 tenths + 9 hundredths

73. _______________________ 8 thousands + 3 hundreds + 5 ones + 5 tenths + 9 hundredths

74. _______________________ 8 thousands + 6 hundreds + 3 tens + 3 ones + 8 tenths + 2 hundredths

75. _______________________ 3 thousands + 1 hundred + 2 tens + 4 ones + 2 tenths + 7 hundredths

76. _______________________ 8 thousands + 3 hundreds + 5 tens + 3 tenths + 4 hundredths

77. _______________________ 2 thousands + 1 hundred + 7 tens + 6 tenths

78. _______________________ 8 thousands + 5 hundreds + 3 ones + 3 tenths + 1 hundredth

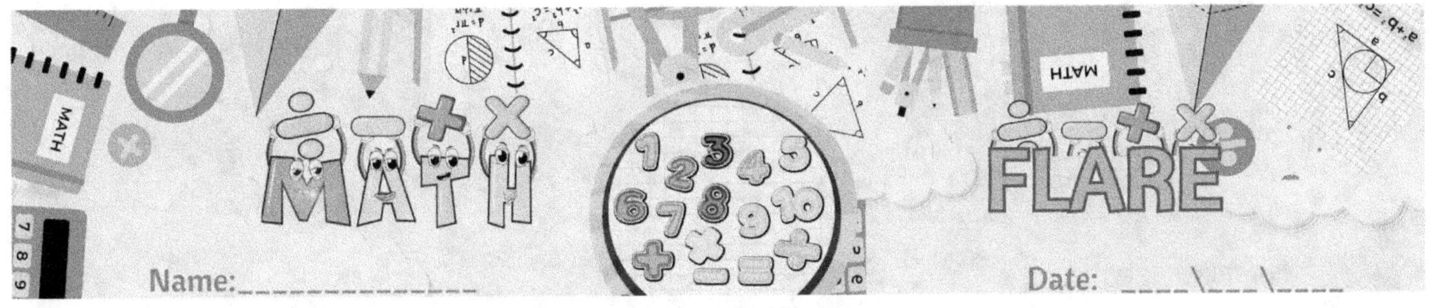

Place Value: Expanded Notation

Provide the expanded notation for each value.

79. 5,007.33 ____

80. 3,247.40 ____

81. 3,075.18 ____

82. 2,738.57 ____

83. 2,865.67 ____

84. 5,359.34 ____________________________

85. 1,817.66 ____________________________

86. 1,745.03 ____________________________

87. 9,208.02 ____________________________

88. 1,182.89 ____________________________

89. 5,307.25 ____________________________

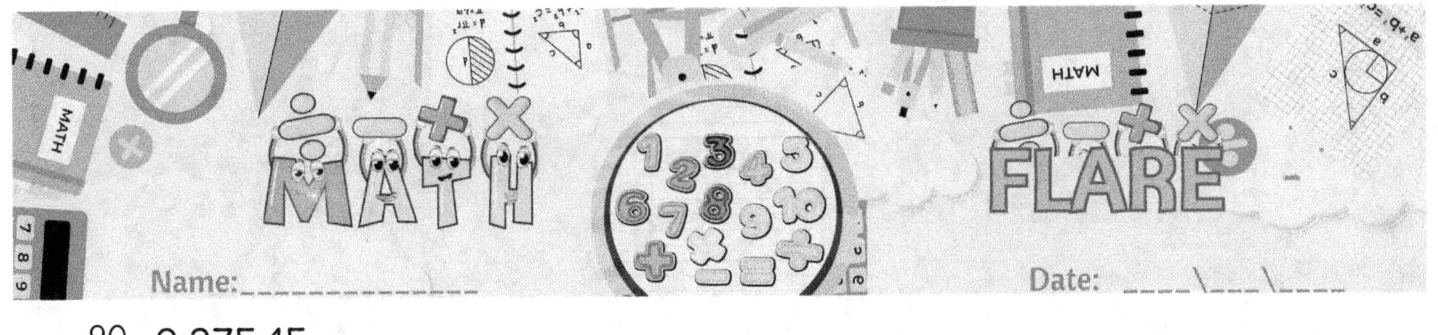

90. 9,275.15 _______________________

91. 1,054.14 _______________________

92. 3,608.31 _______________________

93. 6,626.14 _______________________

94. 6,777.57 _______________________

95. 5,411.45 _______________________

Name:____________________ Date: ____ \ ___ \ ____

96. 3,708.53 ____________________

97. 8,106.10 ____________________

98. 8,105.50 ____________________

99. 9,354.31 ____________________

100. 5,665.76 ____________________

101. 6,485.70 ____________________

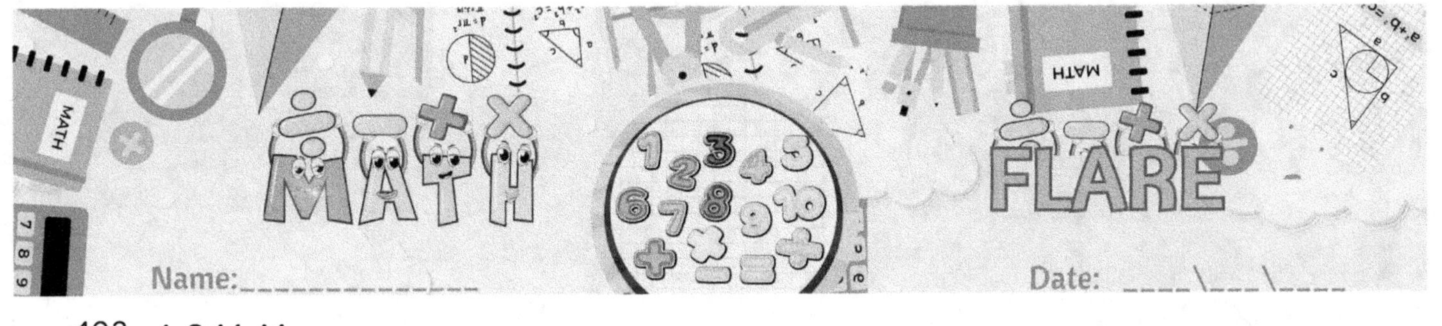

102. 1,011.11 ___________________________

103. 2,072.43 ___________________________

104. 6,275.85 ___________________________

105. 8,206.88 ___________________________

106. 5,731.93 ___________________________

107. 1,104.67 ___________________________

108. 6,987.88 _______________________________

109. 4,981.36 _______________________________

110. 7,275.80 _______________________________

111. 2,527.39 _______________________________

112. 4,702.88 _______________________________

113. 5,651.97 _______________________________

114. 9,970.93 _______________________________

115. 9,955.34 _______________________________

116. 8,794.44 _______________________________

117. 1,585.89 _______________________________

118. 7,147.13 _______________________________

119. 3,672.86 _______________________________

120. 3,908.63 _______________________________
____

121. 7,717.54 _______________________________
____

122. 9,042.42 _______________________________
____

123. 4,398.18 _______________________________
____

124. 4,923.29 _______________________________
____

125. 6,182.64 _______________________________
____

126. 1,148.14

127. 8,728.35

128. 2,528.02

129. 4,222.37

130. 9,415.65

131. 1,244.23

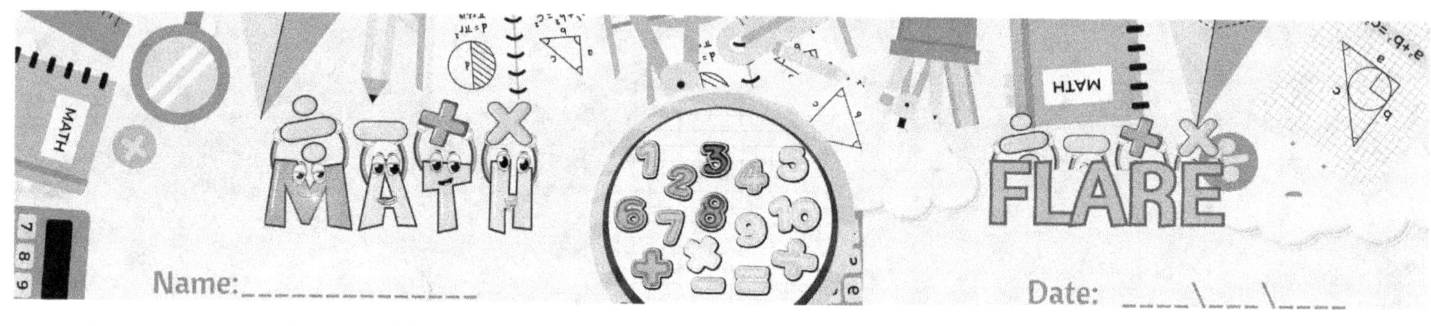

Place Value: Expanded Notation

Provide the expanded notation for each value.

132. _______________________ 40,000 + 600 + 50 + 0.1 + 0.01

133. _______________________ 90,000 + 1,000 + 400 + 80 + 8 + 0.9

134. _______________________ 90,000 + 3,000 + 400 + 10 + 4 + 0.6 + 0.02

135. _______________________ 60,000 + 7,000 + 600 + 10 + 6 + 0.03

136. _______________________ 30,000 + 600 + 40 + 0.7 + 0.09

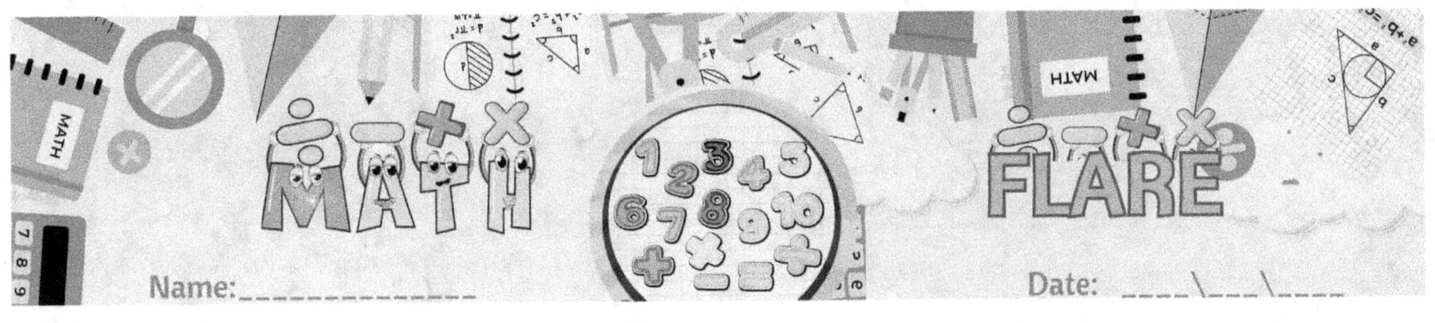

137. _______________________ $10,000 + 6,000 + 600 + 60 + 1 + 0.4 + 0.06$

138. _______________________ $60,000 + 5,000 + 800 + 90 + 7 + 0.2$

139. _______________________ $70,000 + 1,000 + 500 + 20 + 3 + 0.4 + 0.07$

140. _______________________ $60,000 + 800 + 50 + 6 + 0.2 + 0.05$

141. _______________________ $10,000 + 6,000 + 400 + 3 + 0.6 + 0.06$

142. _______________________ $30,000 + 2,000 + 200 + 1 + 0.4 + 0.02$

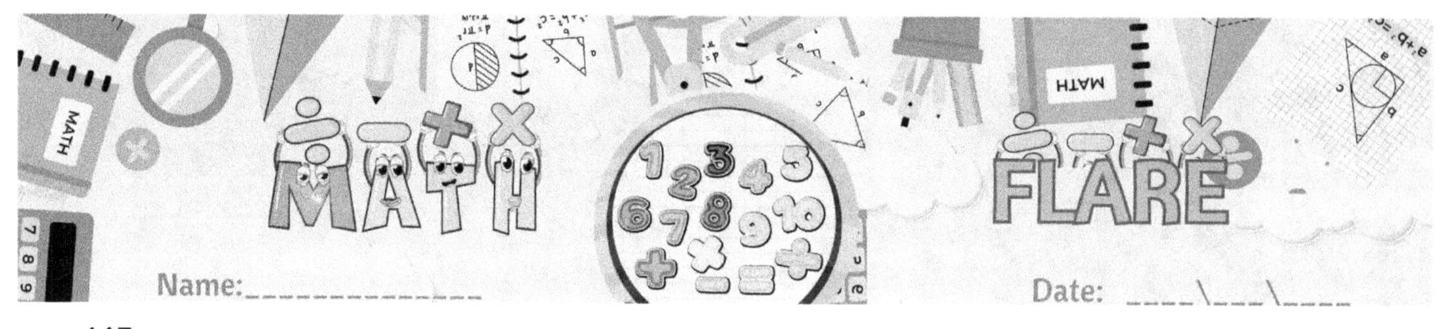

143. _______________________ $60,000 + 2,000 + 10 + 4 + 0.2 + 0.04$

144. _______________________ $80,000 + 300 + 10 + 3 + 0.4 + 0.04$

145. _______________________ $70,000 + 7,000 + 400 + 70 + 7 + 0.5 + 0.04$

146. _______________________ $60,000 + 3,000 + 500 + 10 + 1 + 0.6 + 0.03$

147. _______________________ $70,000 + 9,000 + 500 + 60 + 2 + 0.3 + 0.06$

148. _______________________ $60,000 + 6,000 + 500 + 50 + 1 + 0.08$

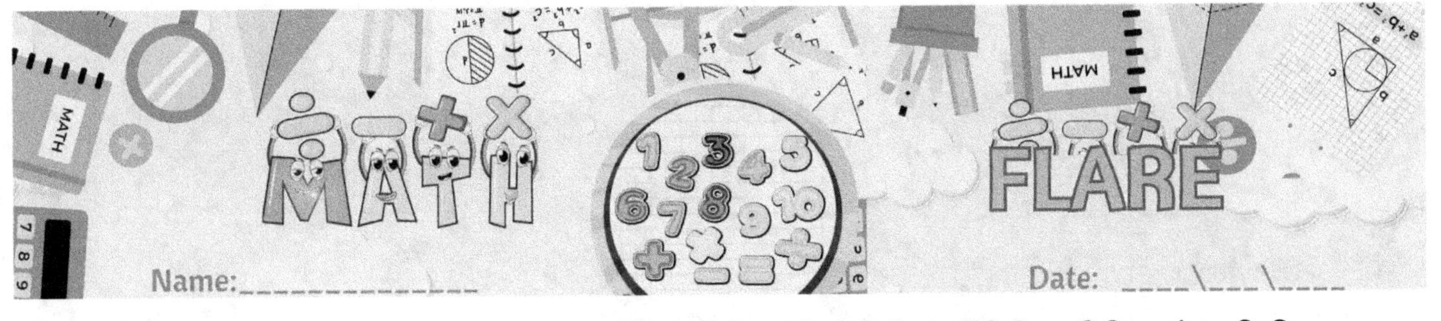

149. _________________________ 60,000 + 8,000 + 200 + 20 + 1 + 0.2 + 0.07

150. _________________________ 60,000 + 6,000 + 100 + 60 + 9 + 0.06

151. _________________________ 30,000 + 1,000 + 200 + 20 + 6 + 0.3 + 0.07

152. _________________________ 10,000 + 9,000 + 500 + 80 + 9 + 0.8 + 0.02

153. _________________________ 50,000 + 4,000 + 300 + 20 + 6 + 0.3

154. _________________________ 60,000 + 4,000 + 400 + 50 + 6 + 0.7 + 0.06

155. _______________________   70,000 + 9,000 + 400 + 80 + 1 + 0.1 + 0.02

156. _______________________   70,000 + 4,000 + 400 + 30 + 1 + 0.7 + 0.01

157. _______________________   60,000 + 6,000 + 100 + 20 + 8 + 0.2 + 0.01

158. _______________________   70,000 + 1,000 + 400 + 90 + 0.3

159. _______________________   10,000 + 900 + 30 + 2 + 0.2 + 0.02

160. _______________________   80,000 + 500 + 80 + 7 + 0.3 + 0.04

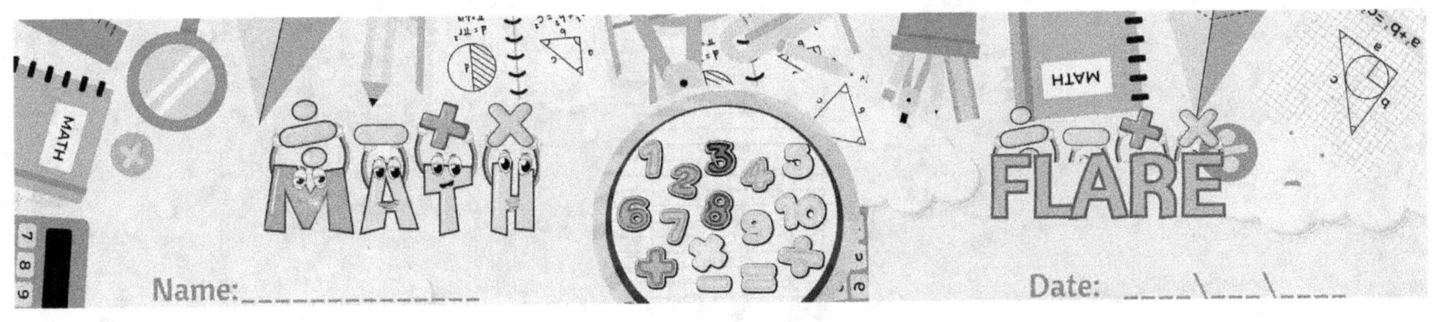

161. _________________________   70,000 + 30 + 4 + 0.7 + 0.07

162. _________________________   80,000 + 5,000 + 700 + 60 + 5 + 0.4 + 0.04

163. _________________________   30,000 + 7,000 + 600 + 50 + 5 + 0.07

164. _________________________   50,000 + 5,000 + 600 + 50 + 6 + 0.1 + 0.04

165. _________________________   70,000 + 300 + 10 + 5 + 0.6 + 0.03

166. _________________________   80,000 + 4,000 + 600 + 20 + 2 + 0.7

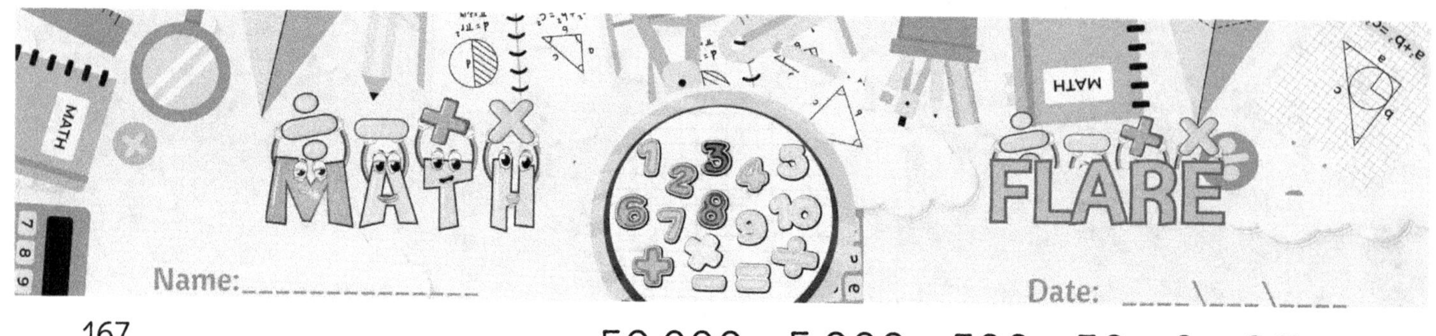

167. _______________________ 50,000 + 5,000 + 500 + 30 + 8 + 0.7 + 0.07

168. _______________________ 60,000 + 3,000 + 100 + 3 + 0.9 + 0.06

169. _______________________ 40,000 + 2,000 + 90 + 3 + 0.2 + 0.01

170. _______________________ 70,000 + 8,000 + 900 + 10 + 2 + 0.5 + 0.07

171. _______________________ 80,000 + 1,000 + 200 + 80 + 2 + 0.9 + 0.01

172. _______________________ 40,000 + 9,000 + 900 + 60 + 0.6 + 0.09

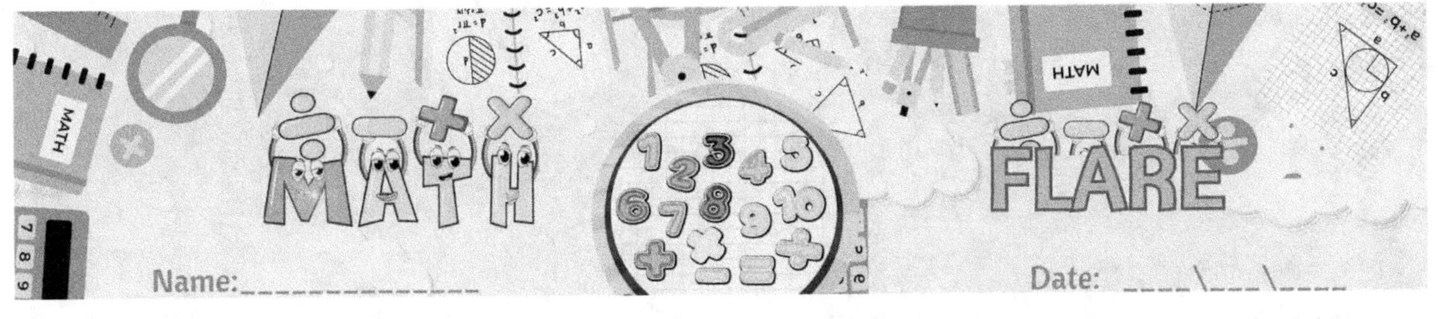

173. ___________________ 90,000 + 9,000 + 900 + 40 + 6 + 0.6 + 0.03

174. ___________________ 70,000 + 5,000 + 800 + 70 + 1 + 0.3 + 0.01

175. ___________________ 30,000 + 2,000 + 600 + 80 + 2 + 0.7 + 0.08

176. ___________________ 50,000 + 4,000 + 900 + 70 + 4 + 0.05

177. ___________________ 30,000 + 8,000 + 400 + 9 + 0.9 + 0.06

178. ___________________ 60,000 + 3,000 + 600 + 60 + 7 + 0.2 + 0.09

179. _________________________ 70,000 + 1,000 + 700 + 50 + 4 + 0.2 + 0.08

180. _________________________ 90,000 + 8,000 + 300 + 10 + 3 + 0.6 + 0.01

181. _________________________ 30,000 + 1,000 + 900 + 10 + 8 + 0.04

182. _________________________ 30,000 + 700 + 30 + 2 + 0.4 + 0.03

183. _________________________ 50,000 + 7,000 + 50 + 7 + 0.8 + 0.04

184. _________________________ 70,000 + 6,000 + 50 + 3 + 0.5 + 0.09

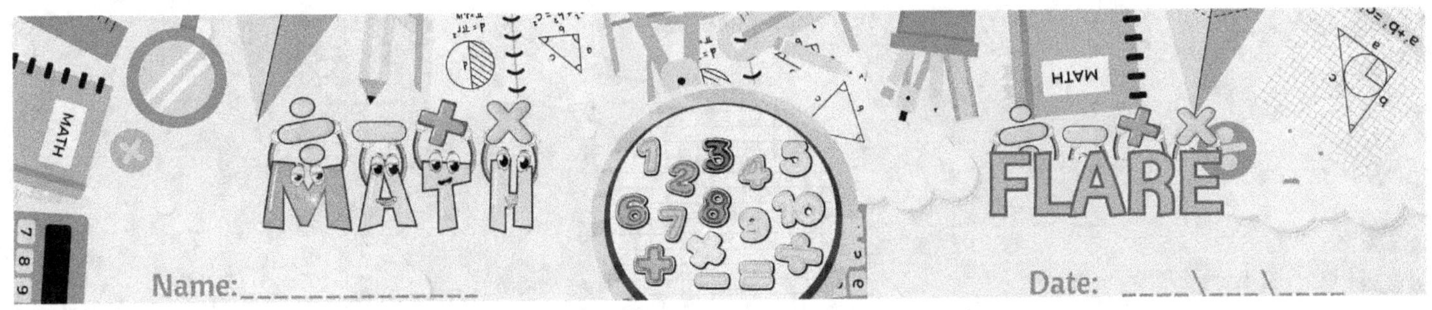

Place Value: Expanded Notation

Provide the expanded notation for each value.

185. 72,930.06 _______________________________

186. 92,851.49 _______________________________

187. 86,322.69 _______________________________

188. 37,032.23 _______________________________

189. 23,933.58 _______________________________

190. 93,183.20 _______________________________

191. 64,511.46 _______________________________

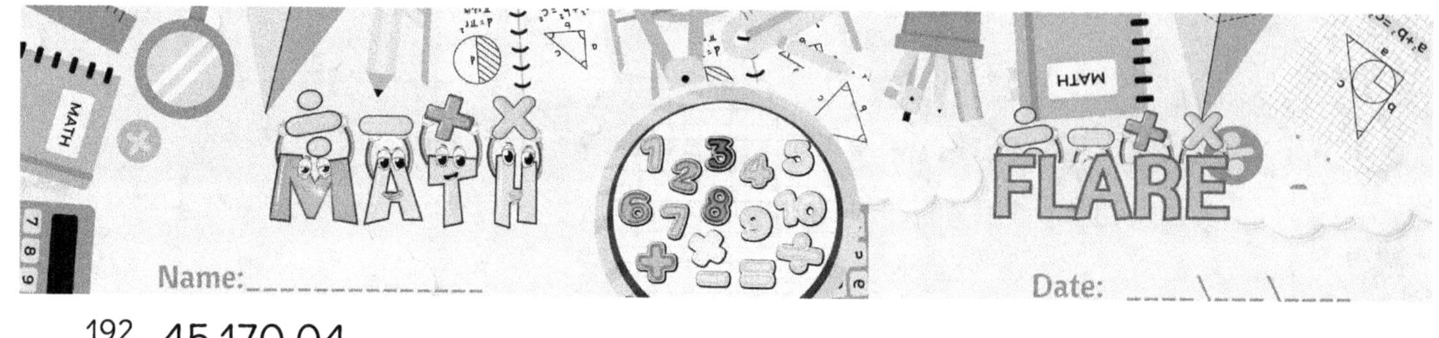

192. 45,170.04 _______________________________

193. 64,965.06 _______________________________

194. 90,935.01 _______________________________

195. 90,820.36 _______________________________

196. 30,637.10 _______________________________

197. 94,545.23 _______________________________

198. 16,358.18 _______________________________

199. 19,997.88 _______________________________

200. 92,853.72 _______________________________

201. 17,972.95 _______________________________

202. 26,458.48 _______________________________

203. 34,457.95 _______________________________

204. 89,307.58 _______________________________

205. 84,885.03 _______________________________

206. 81,264.56 _______________________________

207. 19,642.06 _______________________________

208. 78,453.87 ___________________________

209. 41,774.06 ___________________________

210. 34,507.15 ___________________________

211. 46,021.83 ___________________________

212. 12,461.00 ___________________________

213. 99,734.90 ___________________________

214. 12,617.49 ___________________________

215. 58,669.38 ___________________________

216. 49,302.42 _______________________

217. 38,707.68 _______________________

218. 61,600.36 _______________________

219. 82,724.95 _______________________

220. 77,463.02 _______________________

221. 98,298.88 _______________________

222. 28,506.61 _______________________

223. 49,170.45 _______________________

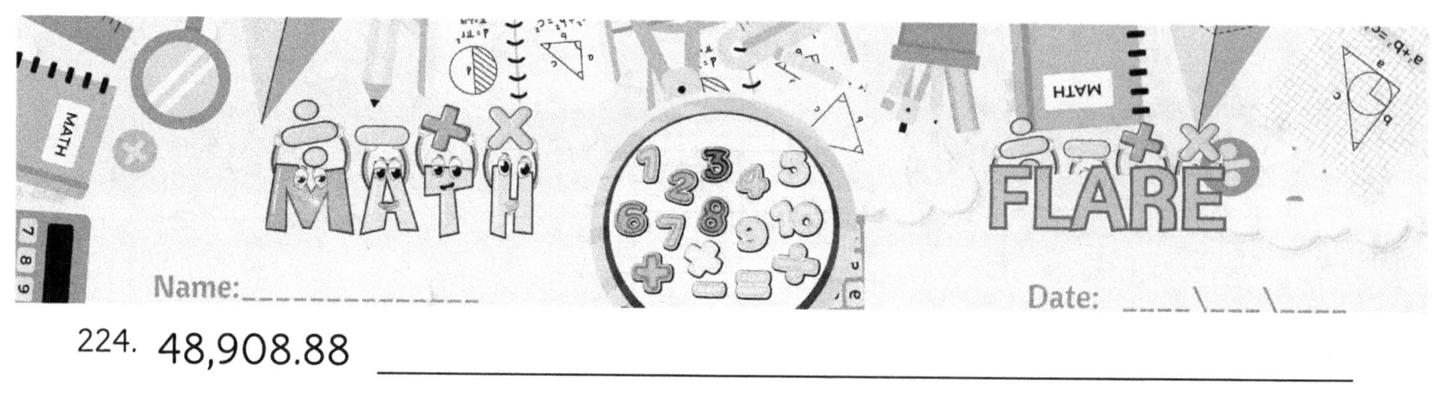

224. 48,908.88 ___________________________

225. 24,401.18 ___________________________

226. 46,112.94 ___________________________

227. 84,994.50 ___________________________

228. 19,011.69 ___________________________

229. 85,049.82 ___________________________

230. 12,045.75 ___________________________

231. 60,427.69 ___________________________

232. 32,051.85 ______________________________

233. 53,669.47 ______________________________

234. 78,899.43 ______________________________

235. 90,340.73 ______________________________

236. 15,459.63 ______________________________

237. 96,273.35 ______________________________

238. 67,749.13 ______________________________

239. 91,167.44 ______________________________

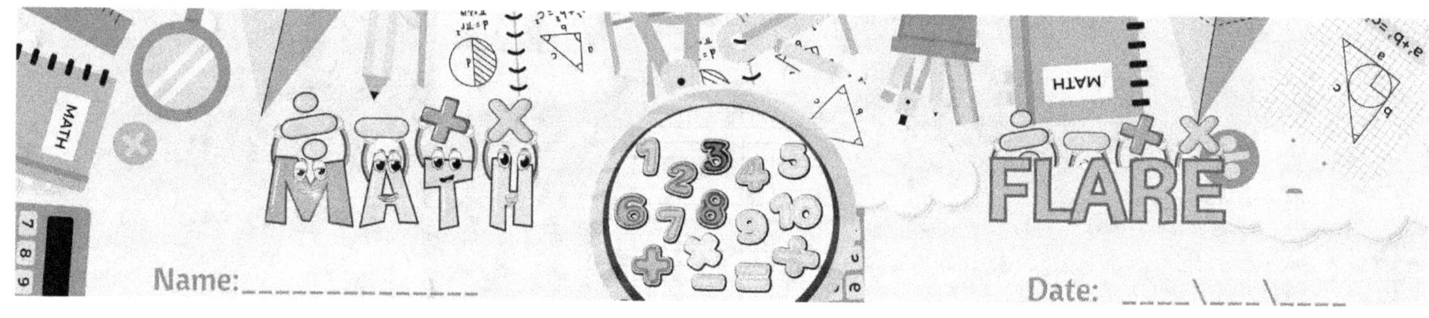

Place Value: Expanded Notation

Provide the expanded notation for each value.

240. _________________________ ninety-one thousand six hundred sixty-five and thirty-eight hundredths

241. _________________________ eighty-three thousand two hundred ten and thirty-nine hundredths

242. _________________________ seventeen thousand eight hundred sixty-eight and ninety-three hundredths

243. _________________________ ninety-five thousand two hundred fifty-eight and ten hundredths

244. _________________________ eighty-nine thousand four hundred twenty-six and twenty-eight hundredths

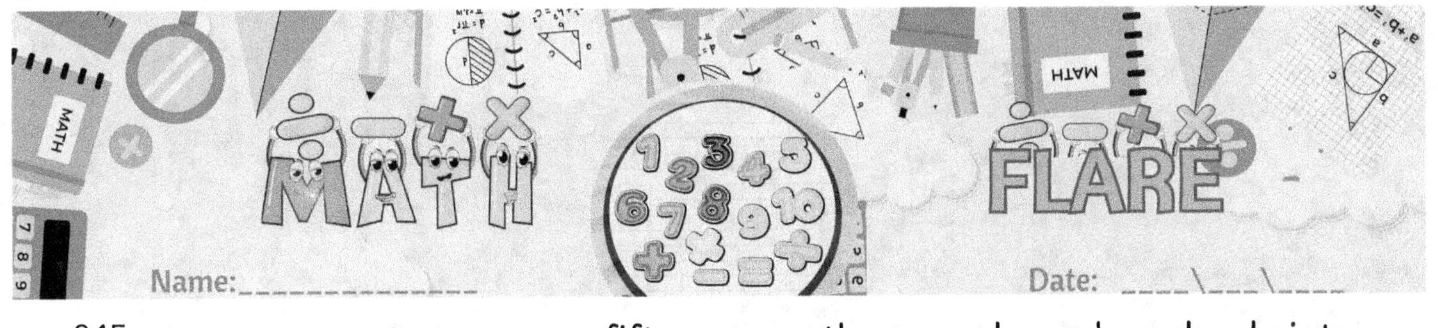

245. _________________________ fifty-seven thousand one hundred sixty -one and ninety-nine hundredths

246. _________________________ sixty-two thousand fifty-one and fourteen hundredths

247. _________________________ forty-five thousand four hundred thirty -four and forty-one hundredths

248. _________________________ sixty-two thousand three hundred forty -eight and twenty-six hundredths

249. _________________________ forty-two thousand two hundred sixty- six and six hundredths

250. _________________________ fifty-one thousand five hundred eighteen and forty-nine hundredths

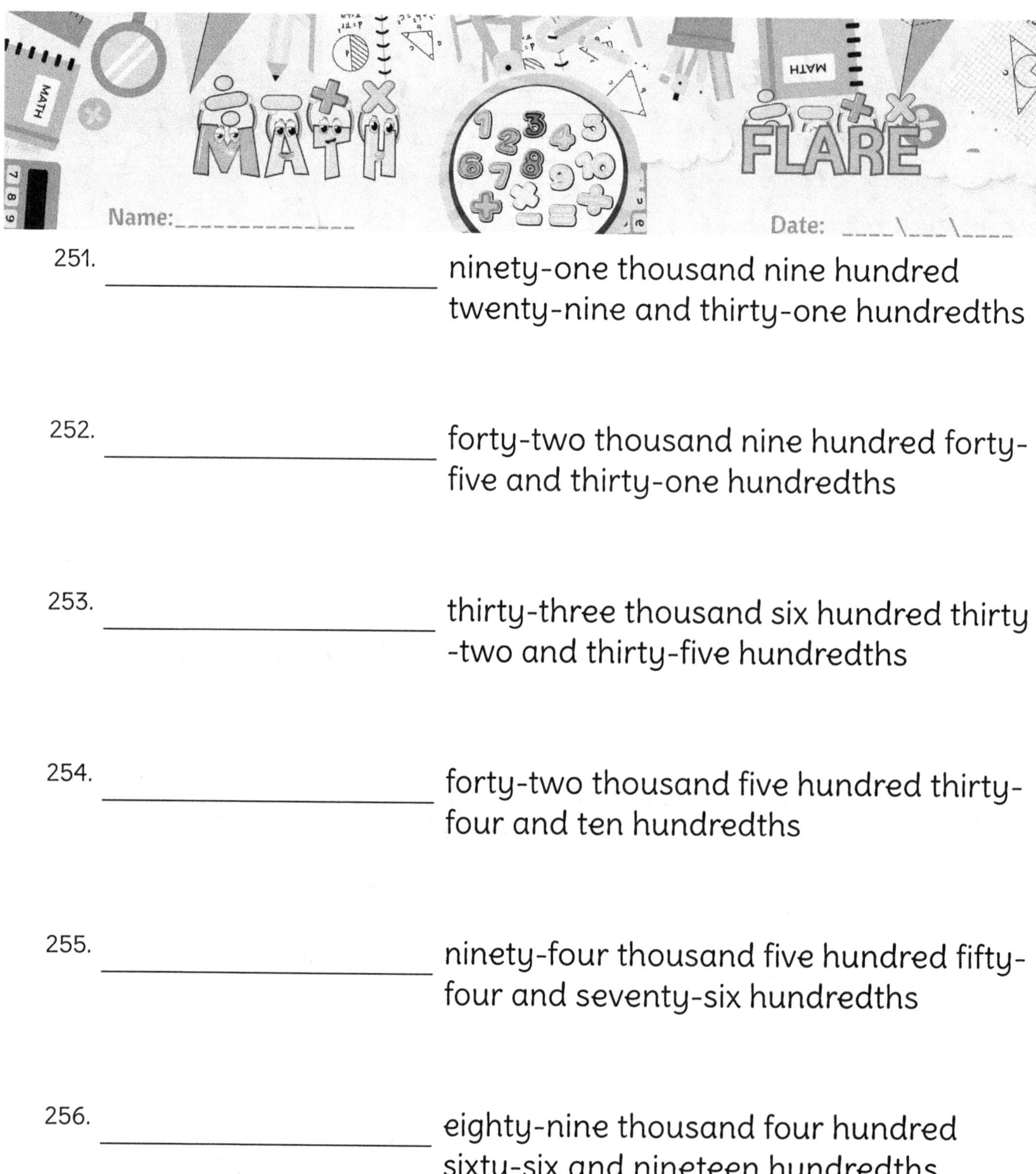

251. __________________________ ninety-one thousand nine hundred twenty-nine and thirty-one hundredths

252. __________________________ forty-two thousand nine hundred forty-five and thirty-one hundredths

253. __________________________ thirty-three thousand six hundred thirty -two and thirty-five hundredths

254. __________________________ forty-two thousand five hundred thirty-four and ten hundredths

255. __________________________ ninety-four thousand five hundred fifty-four and seventy-six hundredths

256. __________________________ eighty-nine thousand four hundred sixty-six and nineteen hundredths

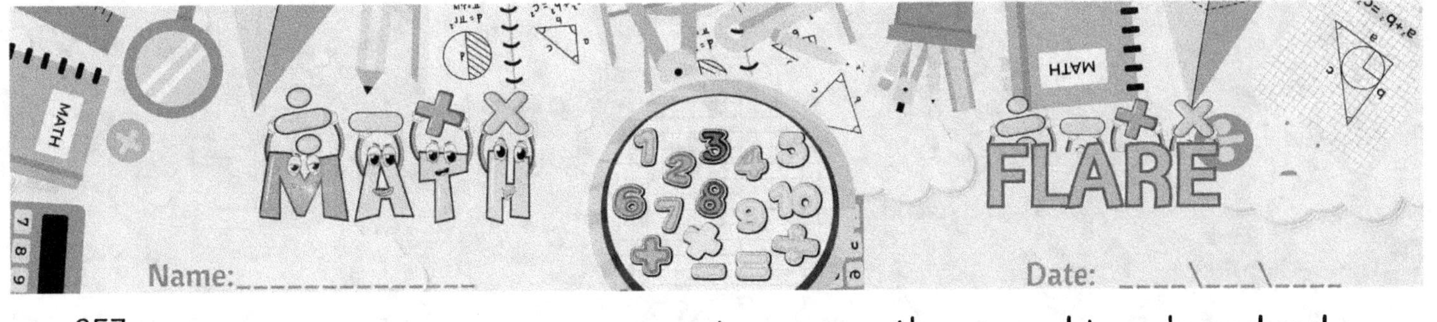

257. _______________________ seventy-seven thousand two hundred eighty-seven and seventy-two hundredths

258. _______________________ eighty-five thousand five hundred forty-eight and eighty-seven hundredths

259. _______________________ seventy-four thousand nine hundred seven and twenty-six hundredths

260. _______________________ forty-eight thousand seven hundred seventy-two and sixty hundredths

261. _______________________ ninety-six thousand two hundred seventy

262. _______________________ ten thousand six hundred thirty and thirty-eight hundredths

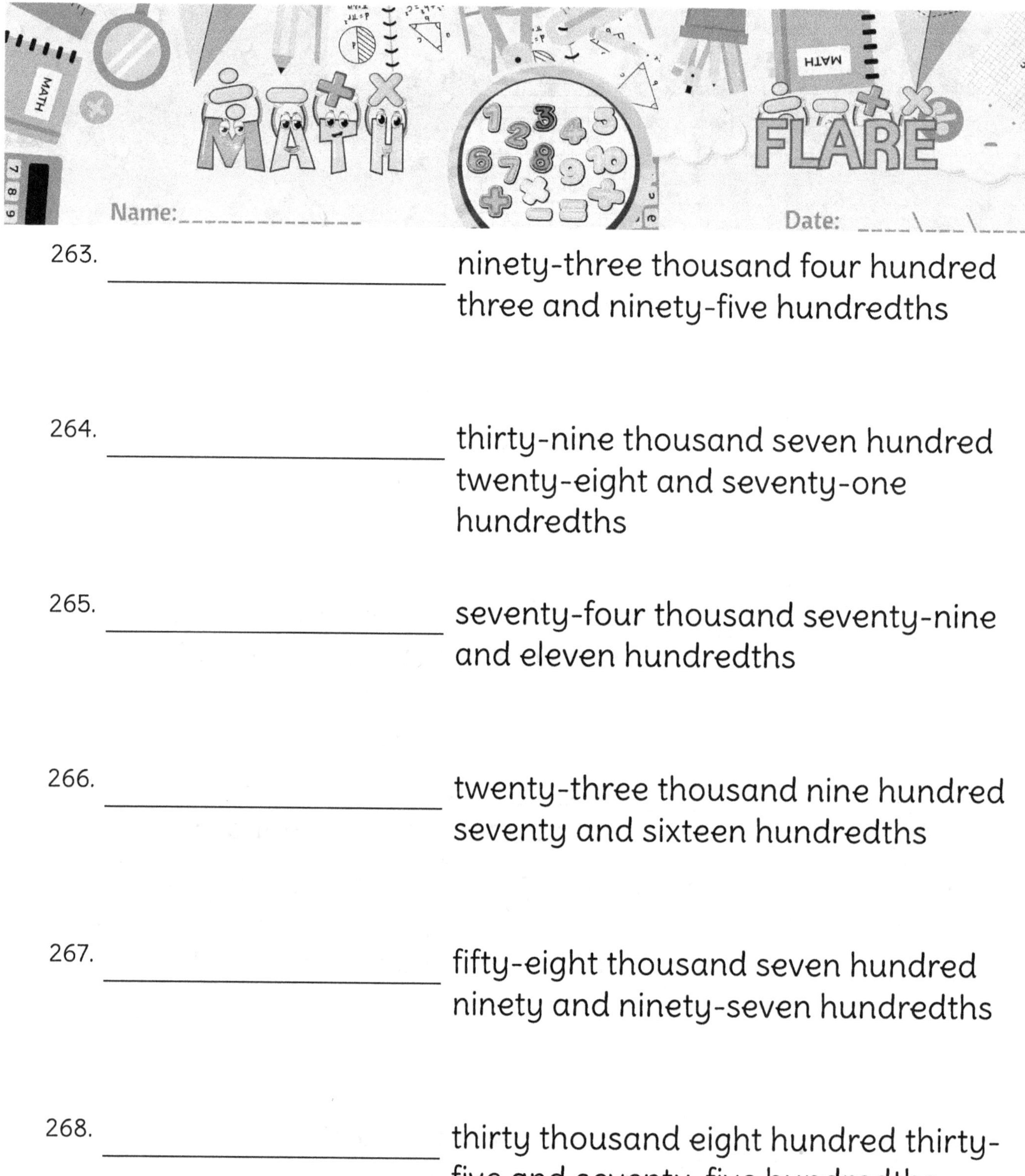

263. _________________________ ninety-three thousand four hundred three and ninety-five hundredths

264. _________________________ thirty-nine thousand seven hundred twenty-eight and seventy-one hundredths

265. _________________________ seventy-four thousand seventy-nine and eleven hundredths

266. _________________________ twenty-three thousand nine hundred seventy and sixteen hundredths

267. _________________________ fifty-eight thousand seven hundred ninety and ninety-seven hundredths

268. _________________________ thirty thousand eight hundred thirty-five and seventy-five hundredths

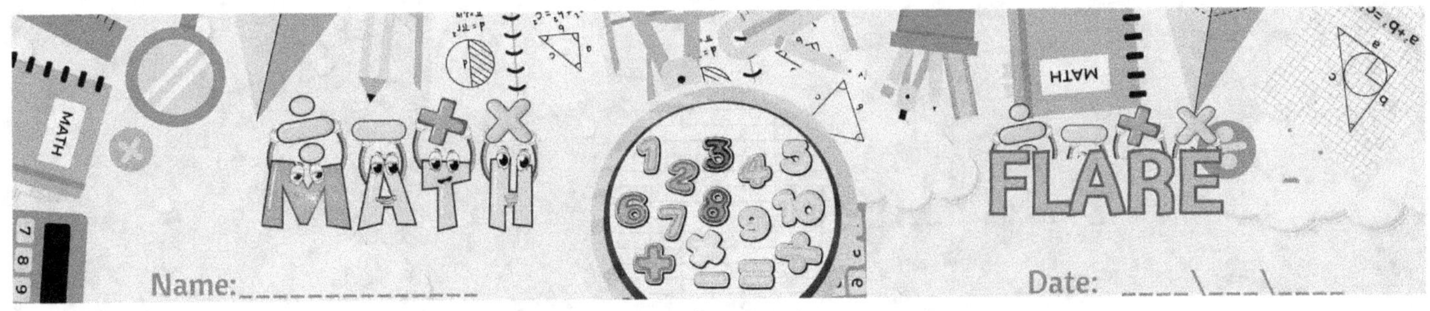

Place Value: Expanded Notation

Provide the expanded notation for each value.

269. 22,275.73 _______________________________

270. 53,210.32 _______________________________

271. 53,028.43 _______________________________

272. 70,958.15 _______________________________

273. 70,432.52 _______________________________

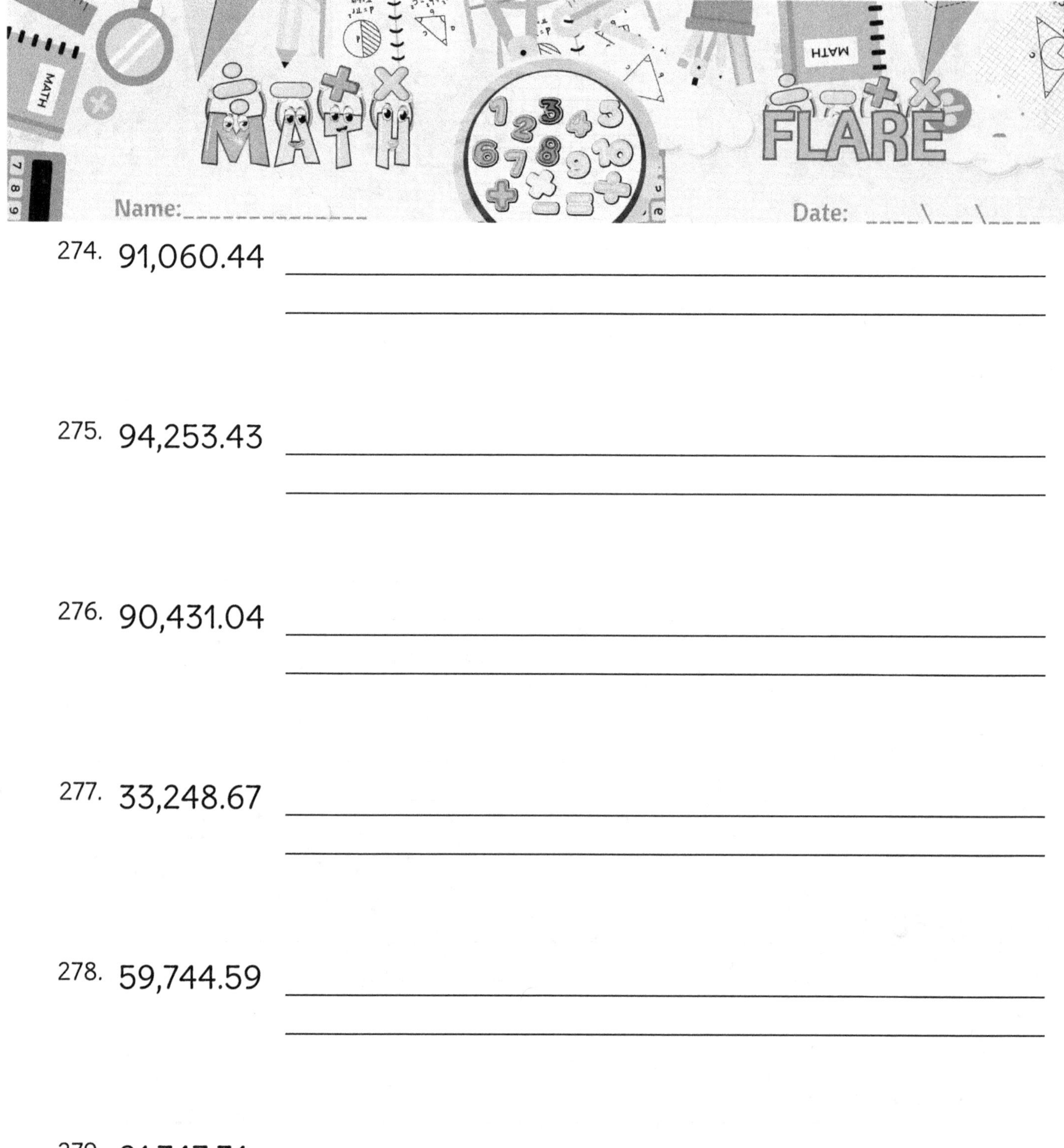

274. 91,060.44

275. 94,253.43

276. 90,431.04

277. 33,248.67

278. 59,744.59

279. 91,747.31

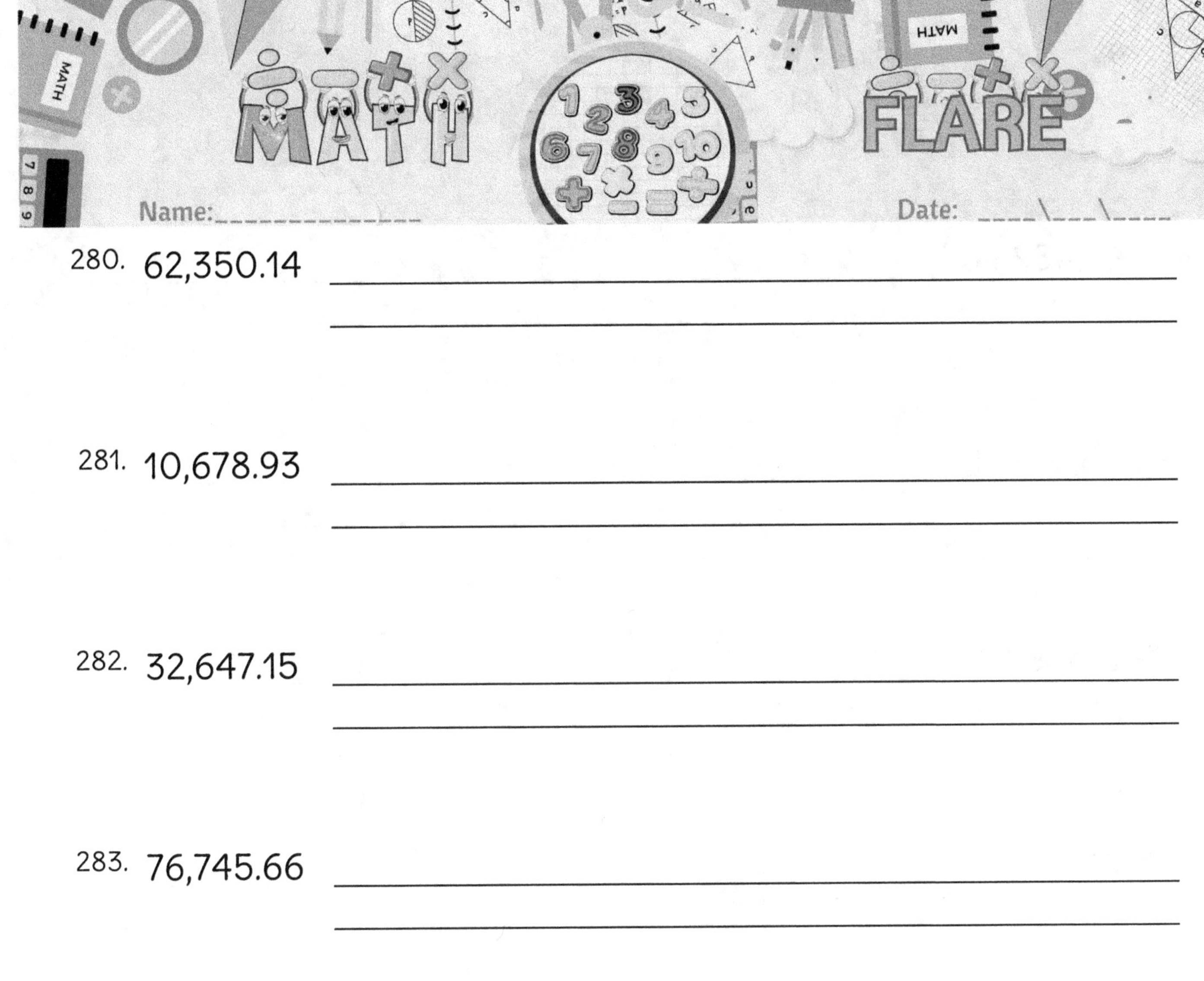

280. 62,350.14 _______________________

281. 10,678.93 _______________________

282. 32,647.15 _______________________

283. 76,745.66 _______________________

284. 43,532.24 _______________________

285. 20,116.37 _______________________

286. 27,482.96 _______________________

287. 98,419.71 _______________________

288. 21,135.87 _______________________

289. 84,345.49 _______________________

290. 10,875.52 _______________________

291. 38,171.89 _______________________

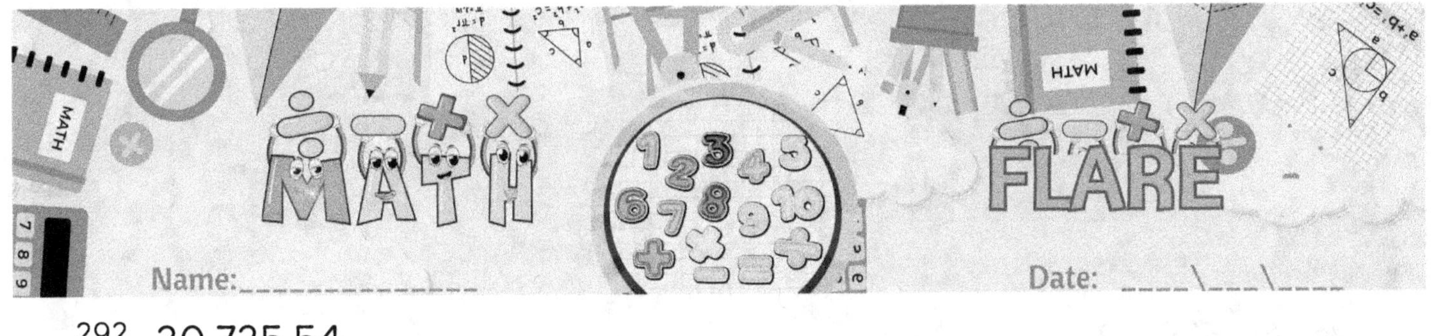

292. 20,725.54 ____________________

293. 92,842.55 ____________________

294. 52,395.84 ____________________

295. 95,395.37 ____________________

296. 82,580.01 ____________________

297. 24,464.96 ____________________

298. 65,529.39 _______________________

299. 25,347.18 _______________________

300. 43,191.83 _______________________

301. 13,260.17 _______________________

302. 24,598.66 _______________________

303. 50,072.53 _______________________

Rounding Numbers
Round to the underlined digit.

304. 890,557.39 = _____________

305. 984,900.58 = _____________

306. 309,711.57 = _____________

307. 725,127.87 = _____________

308. 425,718.99 = _____________

309. 482,806.61 = _____________

310. 141,237.23 = _____________

311. 662,175.30 = _____________

312. 275,431.37 = _____________

313. 938,015.57 = _____________

314. 225,571.17 = _____________

315. 480,936.65 = _____________

316. 736,228.55 = _____________

317. 338,847.12 = _____________

318. 598,71̲7.17 = _____________

319. 2̲96,123.35 = _____________

320. 5̲65,961.48 = _____________

321. 255,504.4̲5 = _____________

322. 476,55̲1.03 = _____________

323. 464,902.5̲5 = _____________

324. 214̲,002.07 = _____________

325. 2̲50,384.30 = _____________

326. 423,02̲8.95 = _____________

327. 781,15̲6.01 = _____________

328. 280,3̲66.86 = _____________

329. 956,65̲0.74 = _____________

330. 216,734.2̲1 = _____________

331. 75̲9,660.82 = _____________

332. 677,1̲92.76 = _____________

333. 443̲,974.15 = _____________

334. 585,554.<u>8</u>3 = _____________   335. 590,899.<u>7</u>3 = _____________

336. 860,802.<u>7</u>3 = _____________   337. 825,746.<u>1</u>9 = _____________

338. 876,8<u>9</u>9.28 = _____________   339. 450,4<u>2</u>1.83 = _____________

340. 891,45<u>2</u>.18 = _____________   341. 5<u>4</u>9,701.78 = _____________

342. 658,<u>4</u>78.17 = _____________   343. 72<u>8</u>,552.13 = _____________

344. 80<u>2</u>,217.71 = _____________   345. 446,5<u>7</u>9.90 = _____________

346. 206,2<u>8</u>7.56 = _____________   347. 269,2<u>3</u>9.86 = _____________

348. 802,<u>8</u>54.40 = _____________   349. 143,<u>0</u>21.74 = _____________

350. 317,725.19 = _____________

351. 586,953.05 = _____________

352. 645,932.48 = _____________

353. 459,170.58 = _____________

354. 687,510.30 = _____________

355. 276,413.91 = _____________

356. 656,050.68 = _____________

357. 781,084.04 = _____________

358. 386,723.30 = _____________

359. 740,173.10 = _____________

360. 661,871.63 = _____________

361. 528,555.55 = _____________

362. 544,761.01 = _____________

363. 469,068.24 = _____________

364. 366,072.40 = _____________

365. 381,576.40 = _____________

366. 984,982.53 = _____________

367. 831,457.20 = _____________

368. 452,460.74 = _____________

369. 634,671.42 = _____________

370. 620,133.91 = _____________

371. 910,482.35 = _____________

372. 461,947.83 = _____________

373. 248,295.35 = _____________

374. 404,671.16 = _____________

375. 116,259.70 = _____________

376. 597,026.26 = _____________

377. 747,998.89 = _____________

378. 662,684.83 = _____________

379. 767,422.15 = _____________

380. 144,096.74 = _____________

381. 253,789.09 = _____________

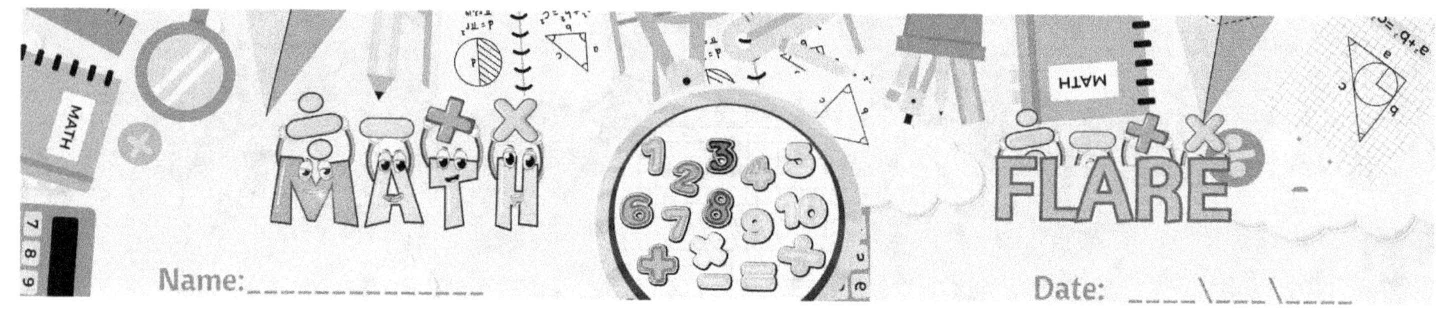

382. 978,3_01.60 = _____________

383. 237,_345.12 = _____________

384. 738,925._55 = _____________

385. 6_29,781.15 = _____________

386. 2_13,728.34 = _____________

387. 318,_022.18 = _____________

388. 756,_463.84 = _____________

389. 4_09,140.92 = _____________

390. 934,_849.04 = _____________

391. 179,7_18.69 = _____________

392. 5_39,022.89 = _____________

393. 2_36,726.18 = _____________

394. 7_88,550.18 = _____________

395. 462,8_96.63 = _____________

396. 1_04,940.77 = _____________

397. 289,40_9.93 = _____________

398. 462,479.73 = _______________

399. 520,641.31 = _______________

400. 461,597.37 = _______________

401. 374,830.35 = _______________

402. 816,779.12 = _______________

403. 268,182.97 = _______________

404. 522,887.82 = _______________

405. 407,242.83 = _______________

406. 225,005.23 = _______________

407. 497,637.13 = _______________

408. 154,499.42 = _______________

409. 671,250.61 = _______________

410. 679,387.63 = _______________

411. 908,051.79 = _______________

412. 218,399.21 = _______________

413. 619,301.14 = _______________

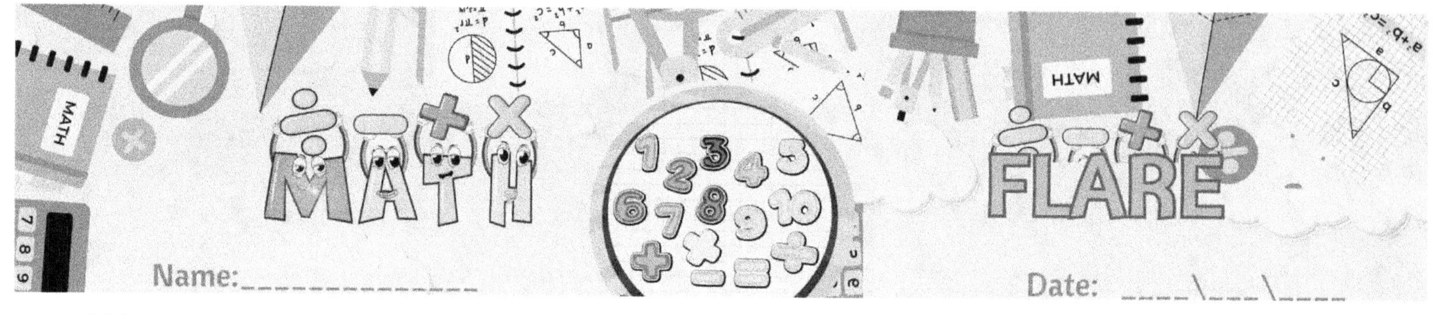

414. 6<u>9</u>6,076.36 = _____________

415. 50<u>8</u>,082.55 = _____________

416. 550,25<u>3</u>.94 = _____________

417. 407,41<u>5</u>.89 = _____________

418. 730,1<u>4</u>2.68 = _____________

419. 736,<u>2</u>91.24 = _____________

420. 267,848.<u>0</u>6 = _____________

421. 766,9<u>6</u>0.34 = _____________

422. 174,99<u>3</u>.36 = _____________

423. 1<u>4</u>3,319.81 = _____________

424. 699,<u>8</u>22.37 = _____________

425. 54<u>0</u>,415.22 = _____________

426. 471,459.46 = _____________

427. 325,2<u>2</u>1.64 = _____________

428. 459,7<u>4</u>5.15 = _____________

429. 941,7<u>7</u>4.52 = _____________

430. 111,318.93 = _______________

431. 407,616.33 = _______________

432. 385,519.15 = _______________

433. 242,043.52 = _______________

434. 405,824.78 = _______________

435. 769,266.38 = _______________

436. 437,009.96 = _______________

437. 810,118.63 = _______________

438. 714,457.29 = _______________

439. 431,682.73 = _______________

440. 504,775.92 = _______________

441. 716,091.20 = _______________

442. 263,522.77 = _______________

443. 185,213.23 = _______________

444. 729,753.28 = _______________

445. 126,797.25 = _______________

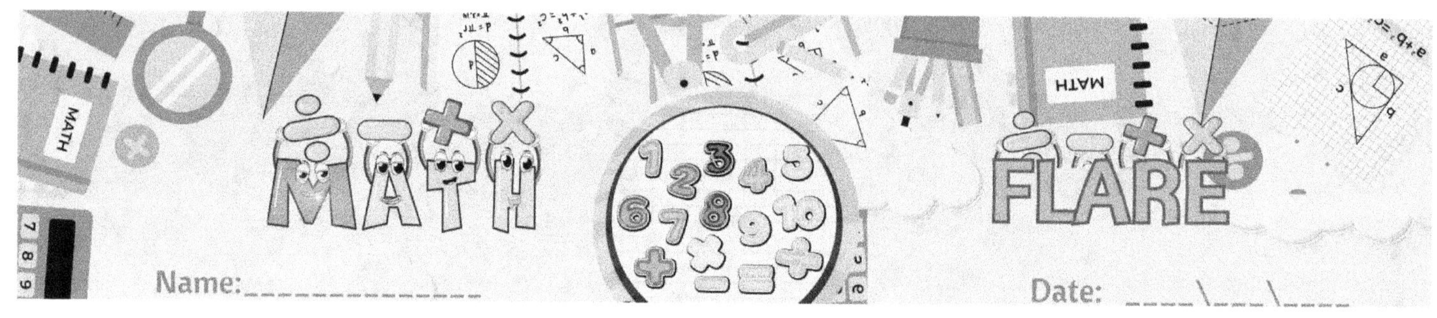

446. 961,319.47 = _______________

447. 919,721.75 = _______________

448. 540,649.82 = _______________

449. 380,467.64 = _______________

450. 912,642.68 = _______________

451. 697,524.88 = _______________

452. 559,267.24 = _______________

453. 726,188.48 = _______________

454. 352,793.25 = _______________

455. 694,637.02 = _______________

456. 299,836.99 = _______________

457. 773,459.30 = _______________

458. 568,360.59 = _______________

459. 982,472.60 = _______________

460. 935,783.36 = _______________

461. 899,783.58 = _______________

ANSWERS

Page 1: Place Value

1. 2 ones
2. 6 thousands
3. 6 ten thousands
4. 7 hundred thousands
5. 6 hundred thousands
6. 4 ones
7. 5 tens
8. 7 ones
9. 0 hundreds
10. 9 thousands
11. 1 one
12. 0 hundreds
13. 0 tens
14. 7 hundred thousands
15. 6 ones
16. 2 hundreds
17. 6 thousands
18. 4 hundred thousands
19. 0 ones
20. 9 tenths
21. 0 tens
22. 1 tenth
23. 8 tens
24. 2 ones
25. 9 tenths
26. 7 ten thousands
27. 8 ones
28. 8 hundred thousands
29. 3 ones
30. 5 tens
31. 4 ten thousands
32. 4 hundredths
33. 0 hundreds
34. 4 ones
35. 4 tenths
36. 3 thousands
37. 7 thousands
38. 2 thousands

39. 6 tenths

40. 4 tenths

41. 0 tens

42. 7 tens

43. 3 hundredths

44. 4 ten thousands

45. 9 ten thousands

46. 1 ten

47. 6 tenths

Page 7:   Place Value: Expanded Notation

48. 5,270.97	49. 2,512.73	50. 1,963.44	51. 1,086.62
52. 8,410.25	53. 5,621.80	54. 7,105.63	55. 5,626.24
56. 3,697.99	57. 3,206.29	58. 9,659.30	59. 3,218.43
60. 3,030.62	61. 1,533.10	62. 3,451.57	63. 2,506.56
64. 4,490.52	65. 4,653.66	66. 6,925.66	67. 9,225.31
68. 8,705.43	69. 4,198.54	70. 6,236.78	71. 3,756.45
72. 5,354.59	73. 8,305.59	74. 8,633.82	75. 3,124.27
76. 8,350.34	77. 2,170.60	78. 8,503.31	

Page 11:   Place Value: Expanded Notation

79. 5 thousands + 7 ones + 3 tenths + 3 hundredths

80. 3 thousands + 2 hundreds + 4 tens + 7 ones + 4 tenths

81. 3 thousands + 7 tens + 5 ones + 1 tenth + 8 hundredths

82. 2 thousands + 7 hundreds + 3 tens + 8 ones + 5 tenths + 7 hundredths

83. 2 thousands + 8 hundreds + 6 tens + 5 ones + 6 tenths + 7 hundredths

84. 5 thousands + 3 hundreds + 5 tens + 9 ones + 3 tenths + 4 hundredths

85. 1 thousand + 8 hundreds + 1 ten + 7 ones + 6 tenths + 6 hundredths

86. 1 thousand + 7 hundreds + 4 tens + 5 ones + 3 hundredths

87. 9 thousands + 2 hundreds + 8 ones + 2 hundredths

88. 1 thousand + 1 hundred + 8 tens + 2 ones + 8 tenths + 9 hundredths

89. 5 thousands + 3 hundreds + 7 ones + 2 tenths + 5 hundredths

90. 9 thousands + 2 hundreds + 7 tens + 5 ones + 1 tenth + 5 hundredths

91. 1 thousand + 5 tens + 4 ones + 1 tenth + 4 hundredths

92. 3 thousands + 6 hundreds + 8 ones + 3 tenths + 1 hundredth

93. 6 thousands + 6 hundreds + 2 tens + 6 ones + 1 tenth + 4 hundredths

94. 6 thousands + 7 hundreds + 7 tens + 7 ones + 5 tenths + 7 hundredths

95. 5 thousands + 4 hundreds + 1 ten + 1 one + 4 tenths + 5 hundredths

96. 3 thousands + 7 hundreds + 8 ones + 5 tenths + 3 hundredths

97. 8 thousands + 1 hundred + 6 ones + 1 tenth

98. 8 thousands + 1 hundred + 5 ones + 5 tenths

99. 9 thousands + 3 hundreds + 5 tens + 4 ones + 3 tenths + 1 hundredth

100. 5 thousands + 6 hundreds + 6 tens + 5 ones + 7 tenths + 6 hundredths

101. 6 thousands + 4 hundreds + 8 tens + 5 ones + 7 tenths

102. 1 thousand + 1 ten + 1 one + 1 tenth + 1 hundredth

103. 2 thousands + 7 tens + 2 ones + 4 tenths + 3 hundredths

104. 6 thousands + 2 hundreds + 7 tens + 5 ones + 8 tenths + 5 hundredths

105. 8 thousands + 2 hundreds + 6 ones + 8 tenths + 8 hundredths

106. 5 thousands + 7 hundreds + 3 tens + 1 one + 9 tenths + 3 hundredths

107. 1 thousand + 1 hundred + 4 ones + 6 tenths + 7 hundredths

108. 6 thousands + 9 hundreds + 8 tens + 7 ones + 8 tenths + 8 hundredths

109. 4 thousands + 9 hundreds + 8 tens + 1 one + 3 tenths + 6 hundredths

110. 7 thousands + 2 hundreds + 7 tens + 5 ones + 8 tenths

111. 2 thousands + 5 hundreds + 2 tens + 7 ones + 3 tenths + 9 hundredths

112. 4 thousands + 7 hundreds + 2 ones + 8 tenths + 8 hundredths

113. 5 thousands + 6 hundreds + 5 tens + 1 one + 9 tenths + 7 hundredths

114. 9 thousands + 9 hundreds + 7 tens + 9 tenths + 3 hundredths

115. 9 thousands + 9 hundreds + 5 tens + 5 ones + 3 tenths + 4 hundredths

116. 8 thousands + 7 hundreds + 9 tens + 4 ones + 4 tenths + 4 hundredths

117. 1 thousand + 5 hundreds + 8 tens + 5 ones + 8 tenths + 9 hundredths

118. 7 thousands + 1 hundred + 4 tens + 7 ones + 1 tenth + 3 hundredths

119. 3 thousands + 6 hundreds + 7 tens + 2 ones + 8 tenths + 6 hundredths

120. 3 thousands + 9 hundreds + 8 ones + 6 tenths + 3 hundredths

121. 7 thousands + 7 hundreds + 1 ten + 7 ones + 5 tenths + 4 hundredths

122. 9 thousands + 4 tens + 2 ones + 4 tenths + 2 hundredths

123. 4 thousands + 3 hundreds + 9 tens + 8 ones + 1 tenth + 8 hundredths

124. 4 thousands + 9 hundreds + 2 tens + 3 ones + 2 tenths + 9 hundredths

125. 6 thousands + 1 hundred + 8 tens + 2 ones + 6 tenths + 4 hundredths

126. 1 thousand + 1 hundred + 4 tens + 8 ones + 1 tenth + 4 hundredths

127. 8 thousands + 7 hundreds + 2 tens + 8 ones + 3 tenths + 5 hundredths

128. 2 thousands + 5 hundreds + 2 tens + 8 ones + 2 hundredths

129. 4 thousands + 2 hundreds + 2 tens + 2 ones + 3 tenths + 7 hundredths

130. 9 thousands + 4 hundreds + 1 ten + 5 ones + 6 tenths + 5 hundredths

131. 1 thousand + 2 hundreds + 4 tens + 4 ones + 2 tenths + 3 hundredths

Page 20:   Place Value: Expanded Notation

132. 40,650.11	133. 91,488.90	134. 93,414.62	135. 67,616.03
136. 30,640.79	137. 16,661.46	138. 65,897.20	139. 71,523.47
140. 60,856.25	141. 16,403.66	142. 32,201.42	143. 62,014.24
144. 80,313.44	145. 77,477.54	146. 63,511.63	147. 79,562.36
148. 66,551.08	149. 68,221.27	150. 66,169.06	151. 31,226.37
152. 19,589.82	153. 54,326.30	154. 64,456.76	155. 79,481.12
156. 74,431.71	157. 66,128.21	158. 71,490.30	159. 10,932.22
160. 80,587.34	161. 70,034.77	162. 85,765.44	163. 37,655.07
164. 55,656.14	165. 70,315.63	166. 84,622.70	167. 55,538.77
168. 63,103.96	169. 42,093.21	170. 78,912.57	171. 81,282.91
172. 49,960.69	173. 99,946.63	174. 75,871.31	175. 32,682.78
176. 54,974.05	177. 38,409.96	178. 63,667.29	179. 71,754.28
180. 98,313.61	181. 31,918.04	182. 30,732.43	183. 57,057.84
184. 76,053.59			

Page 29: Place Value: Expanded Notation

185. 70,000 + 2,000 + 900 + 30 + 0.06

186. 90,000 + 2,000 + 800 + 50 + 1 + 0.4 + 0.09

187. 80,000 + 6,000 + 300 + 20 + 2 + 0.6 + 0.09

188. 30,000 + 7,000 + 30 + 2 + 0.2 + 0.03

189. 20,000 + 3,000 + 900 + 30 + 3 + 0.5 + 0.08

190. 90,000 + 3,000 + 100 + 80 + 3 + 0.2

191. 60,000 + 4,000 + 500 + 10 + 1 + 0.4 + 0.06

192. 40,000 + 5,000 + 100 + 70 + 0.04

193. 60,000 + 4,000 + 900 + 60 + 5 + 0.06

194. 90,000 + 900 + 30 + 5 + 0.01

195. 90,000 + 800 + 20 + 0.3 + 0.06

196. 30,000 + 600 + 30 + 7 + 0.1

197. 90,000 + 4,000 + 500 + 40 + 5 + 0.2 + 0.03

198. 10,000 + 6,000 + 300 + 50 + 8 + 0.1 + 0.08

199. 10,000 + 9,000 + 900 + 90 + 7 + 0.8 + 0.08

200. 90,000 + 2,000 + 800 + 50 + 3 + 0.7 + 0.02

201. 10,000 + 7,000 + 900 + 70 + 2 + 0.9 + 0.05

202. 20,000 + 6,000 + 400 + 50 + 8 + 0.4 + 0.08

203. 30,000 + 4,000 + 400 + 50 + 7 + 0.9 + 0.05

204. 80,000 + 9,000 + 300 + 7 + 0.5 + 0.08

205. 80,000 + 4,000 + 800 + 80 + 5 + 0.03

206. 80,000 + 1,000 + 200 + 60 + 4 + 0.5 + 0.06

207. 10,000 + 9,000 + 600 + 40 + 2 + 0.06

208. 70,000 + 8,000 + 400 + 50 + 3 + 0.8 + 0.07

209. 40,000 + 1,000 + 700 + 70 + 4 + 0.06

210. 30,000 + 4,000 + 500 + 7 + 0.1 + 0.05

211. 40,000 + 6,000 + 20 + 1 + 0.8 + 0.03

212. 10,000 + 2,000 + 400 + 60 + 1

213. 90,000 + 9,000 + 700 + 30 + 4 + 0.9

214. 10,000 + 2,000 + 600 + 10 + 7 + 0.4 + 0.09

215. 50,000 + 8,000 + 600 + 60 + 9 + 0.3 + 0.08

216. 40,000 + 9,000 + 300 + 2 + 0.4 + 0.02

217. 30,000 + 8,000 + 700 + 7 + 0.6 + 0.08

218. 60,000 + 1,000 + 600 + 0.3 + 0.06

219. 80,000 + 2,000 + 700 + 20 + 4 + 0.9 + 0.05

220. 70,000 + 7,000 + 400 + 60 + 3 + 0.02

221. 90,000 + 8,000 + 200 + 90 + 8 + 0.8 + 0.08

222. 20,000 + 8,000 + 500 + 6 + 0.6 + 0.01

223. 40,000 + 9,000 + 100 + 70 + 0.4 + 0.05

224. 40,000 + 8,000 + 900 + 8 + 0.8 + 0.08

225. 20,000 + 4,000 + 400 + 1 + 0.1 + 0.08

226. 40,000 + 6,000 + 100 + 10 + 2 + 0.9 + 0.04

227. 80,000 + 4,000 + 900 + 90 + 4 + 0.5

228. 10,000 + 9,000 + 10 + 1 + 0.6 + 0.09

229. 80,000 + 5,000 + 40 + 9 + 0.8 + 0.02

230. 10,000 + 2,000 + 40 + 5 + 0.7 + 0.05

231. 60,000 + 400 + 20 + 7 + 0.6 + 0.09

232. 30,000 + 2,000 + 50 + 1 + 0.8 + 0.05

233. 50,000 + 3,000 + 600 + 60 + 9 + 0.4 + 0.07

234. 70,000 + 8,000 + 800 + 90 + 9 + 0.4 + 0.03

235. 90,000 + 300 + 40 + 0.7 + 0.03

236. 10,000 + 5,000 + 400 + 50 + 9 + 0.6 + 0.03

237. 90,000 + 6,000 + 200 + 70 + 3 + 0.3 + 0.05

238. 60,000 + 7,000 + 700 + 40 + 9 + 0.1 + 0.03

239. 90,000 + 1,000 + 100 + 60 + 7 + 0.4 + 0.04

Page 36:   Place Value: Expanded Notation

240. 91,665.38	241. 83,210.39	242. 17,868.93	243. 95,258.10
244. 89,426.28	245. 57,161.99	246. 62,051.14	247. 45,434.41
248. 62,348.26	249. 42,266.06	250. 51,518.49	251. 91,929.31
252. 42,945.31	253. 33,632.35	254. 42,534.10	255. 94,554.76
256. 89,466.19	257. 77,287.72	258. 85,548.87	259. 74,907.26
260. 48,772.60	261. 96,270.00	262. 10,630.38	263. 93,403.95

264. 39,728.71   265. 74,079.11   266. 23,970.16   267. 58,790.97

268. 30,835.75

Page 41: Place Value: Expanded Notation

269. twenty-two thousand two hundred seventy-five and seventy-three hundredths

270. fifty-three thousand two hundred ten and thirty-two hundredths

271. fifty-three thousand twenty-eight and forty-three hundredths

272. seventy thousand nine hundred fifty-eight and fifteen hundredths

273. seventy thousand four hundred thirty-two and fifty-two hundredths

274. ninety-one thousand sixty and forty-four hundredths

275. ninety-four thousand two hundred fifty-three and forty-three hundredths

276. ninety thousand four hundred thirty-one and four hundredths

277. thirty-three thousand two hundred forty-eight and sixty-seven hundredths

278. fifty-nine thousand seven hundred forty-four and fifty-nine hundredths

279. ninety-one thousand seven hundred forty-seven and thirty-one hundredths

280. sixty-two thousand three hundred fifty and fourteen hundredths

281. ten thousand six hundred seventy-eight and ninety-three hundredths

282. thirty-two thousand six hundred forty-seven and fifteen hundredths

283. seventy-six thousand seven hundred forty-five and sixty-six hundredths

284. forty-three thousand five hundred thirty-two and twenty-four hundredths

285. twenty thousand one hundred sixteen and thirty-seven hundredths

286. twenty-seven thousand four hundred eighty-two and ninety-six hundredths

287. ninety-eight thousand four hundred nineteen and seventy-one hundredths

288. twenty-one thousand one hundred thirty-five and eighty-seven hundredths

289. eighty-four thousand three hundred forty-five and forty-nine hundredths

290. ten thousand eight hundred seventy-five and fifty-two hundredths

291. thirty-eight thousand one hundred seventy-one and eighty-nine hundredths

292. twenty thousand seven hundred twenty-five and fifty-four hundredths

293. ninety-two thousand eight hundred forty-two and fifty-five hundredths

294. fifty-two thousand three hundred ninety-five and eighty-four hundredths

295. ninety-five thousand three hundred ninety-five and thirty-seven hundredths

296. eighty-two thousand five hundred eighty and one hundredth

297. twenty-four thousand four hundred sixty-four and ninety-six hundredths

298. sixty-five thousand five hundred twenty-nine and thirty-nine hundredths

299. twenty-five thousand three hundred forty-seven and eighteen hundredths

300. forty-three thousand one hundred ninety-one and eighty-three hundredths

301. thirteen thousand two hundred sixty and seventeen hundredths

302. twenty-four thousand five hundred ninety-eight and sixty-six hundredths

303. fifty thousand seventy-two and fifty-three hundredths

Page 47: Rounding Numbers

304. 890,557	305. 985,000	306. 310,000	307. 725,100
308. 426,000	309. 482,810	310. 141,000	311. 660,000
312. 275,400	313. 940,000	314. 225,571.2	315. 480,937
316. 740,000	317. 339,000	318. 599,000	319. 300,000
320. 570,000	321. 255,504.5	322. 476,551	323. 464,902.6
324. 214,000	325. 250,000	326. 423,029	327. 781,156
328. 280,400	329. 956,651	330. 216,734.2	331. 760,000
332. 677,200	333. 444,000	334. 585,554.8	335. 590,899.7
336. 860,802.7	337. 825,746	338. 876,900	339. 450,420
340. 891,452	341. 550,000	342. 658,500	343. 729,000
344. 802,000	345. 446,580	346. 206,290	347. 269,240

348. 802,900

349. 143,000

350. 317,725

351. 586,953.1

352. 646,000

353. 460,000

354. 687,510.3

355. 276,413.9

356. 656,100

357. 781,000

358. 386,720

359. 740,170

360. 661,870

361. 529,000

362. 544,761

363. 469,070

364. 366,070

365. 380,000

366. 984,983

367. 830,000

368. 450,000

369. 634,671.4

370. 620,133.9

371. 910,500

372. 461,950

373. 248,300

374. 405,000

375. 116,259.7

376. 597,000

377. 748,000

378. 662,680

379. 767,420

380. 144,100

381. 254,000

382. 978,300

383. 237,000

384. 738,925.6

385. 630,000

386. 210,000

387. 318,000

388. 756,500

389. 410,000

390. 934,800

391. 179,720

392. 540,000

393. 240,000

394. 790,000

395. 462,900

396. 100,000

397. 289,410

398. 462,480

399. 521,000

400. 461,597.4

401. 374,800

402. 816,800

403. 268,200

404. 522,900

405. 407,200

406. 225,000

407. 497,640

408. 154,499.4

409. 671,250.6

410. 679,400

411. 908,051.8

412. 218,399

413. 620,000

414. 700,000

415. 508,000

416. 550,254

417. 407,416

418. 730,140

419. 736,300

420. 267,848.1

421. 766,960

422. 174,993

423. 140,000

424. 699,800

425. 540,000

426. 471,000

427. 325,220

428. 459,750

429. 941,770

430. 111,318.9

431. 407,620

432. 385,519.2

433. 242,000

434. 405,825

435. 770,000

436. 437,010

437. 810,118.6

438. 714,457

439. 431,680

440. 504,776

441. 716,100

442. 264,000

443. 185,210

444. 729,750

445. 126,800

446. 961,319.5

447. 920,000

448. 540,649.8

449. 380,468

450. 912,643

451. 698,000

452. 559,000

453. 730,000

454. 353,000

455. 694,600

456. 299,837

457. 773,500

458. 568,360.6

459. 982,000

460. 940,000

461. 899,783.6